COMMUNICATION AND INFORMATION ECONOMICS

New Perspectives

Edited by

MEHEROO JUSSAWALLA
East-West Center
Honolulu
Hawaii
U.S.A.

and

HELENE EBENFIELD
National Science Foundation
Washington D.C.
U.S.A.

With a Foreword by

KENNETH E. BOULDING

1984

NORTH-HOLLAND
AMSTERDAM · NEW YORK · OXFORD

ISBN: 0 444 87589 1

Published by:
ELSEVIER SCIENCE PUBLISHERS B.V.
P.O. Box 1991
1000 BZ Amsterdam
The Netherlands

Sole distributors for the U.S.A. and Canada:
ELSEVIER SCIENCE PUBLISHING COMPANY, INC.
52 Vanderbilt Avenue
New York, N.Y. 10017
U.S.A.

Library of Congress Cataloging in Publication Data

Main entry under title:

Communication and information economics.

(Information research and resource reports ; v. 5)
Bibliography: p.
1. Telecommunication--Addresses, essays, lectures.
I. Jussawalla, Meheroo, 1923- . II. Ebenfield, Helene. III. Title: Information economics.
IV. Series.
HE7631.C56 1984 384'.041 84-13596
ISBN 0-444-87589-1 (U.S.)

PRINTED IN THE NETHERLANDS

COMMUNICATION AND INFORMATION ECONOMICS
New Perspectives

INFORMATION RESEARCH AND RESOURCE REPORTS

VOLUME 5

Editors-in-Chief:

N. SZYPERSKI

and

F. WINKELHAGE

Gesellschaft für Mathematik
und Datenverarbeitung mbH Bonn

NORTH-HOLLAND
AMSTERDAM · NEW YORK · OXFORD

CONTENTS

FOREWORD

A NOTE ON INFORMATION, KNOWLEDGE, AND PRODUCTION

Kenneth E. Boulding
University of Colorado

It is very fashionable now to regard the present as the information age. And while there are usually good reasons for things being fashionable, there are also dangers involved, especially the neglect of what may not be so fashionable. The good reason behind the fashion for information is that since the development of information theory by Shannon and Weaver, it has become clear that the universe is not just composed of matter and energy, but that the evolutionary process in it is a process fundamentally in information and related concepts, with matter and energy being mainly significant as coders of information. The same information can be coded in many different ways, in structures both of matter and of energy.

Information in the Shannon-Weaver sense, however, which I have sometimes called "Bell Telephone information," is only the most elementary of a whole series of concepts. It is a metaphor ot say that Bell Telephone information is what is surprising, but it is a fairly good metaphor, for the concept is closely related to the improbability of structures.

When we look at biological evolution, however, we have to go beyond the Bell Telephone concept into what can be called know-how, which is what the divided cell or the fertilized egg have. Two fertilized eggs can have the same amount of information in terms of bits, but one knows how to make a hippopotamus and the other knows how to make a giraffe. It is clear that know-how goes beyond the simple information concept, although it is very hard to identify it and to quantify. Indeed, I suspect it cannot be quantified, simply because it has such a very large number of dimensions. Quantification always involves losing information and crunching down an n-dimensional structure into a one-dimensional structure, as we see, for instance, in such a concept as the GNP. Two countries can have the same GNP, but in one the structure may involve very unequal distribution, a large war industry, the production of palaces; in the other, distribution may be fairly equal, and the products may consist of things that are useful to the ordinary mass of human beings. Quantification here is simply a curtain pulled over the truth.

With the development of the human race (and perhaps a little earlier), a new structure emerges, which we can call know-what. This consists of the structures in the nervous system which presumably map into some kind of images in the "mind," which also map into structures in the "real world," whatever that is. Know-what is very different from know-how. The fertilized egg certainly has the know-how to make whatever organism it knows how to make, but it is very doubtful that it knows what it is doing. The remarkable thing about know-what is that it creates know-how, as we see with the fantastic burgeoning of human artifacts under the influence of a science-based technology. Science, fundamentally, deals with know-what, and this enormously increases know-how. The alchemists would never have produced plastics any more than they produced gold because their know-what was so imperfect. The elements are not earth, air, fire, and water, but not until we discovered the chemical elements and the periodic table were we able to create a chemical industry. Similarly, electricity was just playful magic until Ohm, Farraday, and Clerk-Maxwell created the know-what that then gave us the know-how to make power stations, electric power, and light.

One can even go beyond know-what into know-whether. This involves the evaluative structure of the human mind which enables us to make decisions and choices among different images of the future. Human behavior cannot be explained without this further development in the hierarchy that starts with simple information. This actually goes back a long way in evolution. Even the amoeba knows whether to absorb a piece of grit or a piece of food.

What does all this mean for economics? It means, first, that we have to revise our theories of production. I have argued that land, labor, and capital, even if we add Alfred Marshall's "organization," are hoplelessly heterogeneous aggregates, much on a par with earth, air, fire, and water. And that what might be called a cookbook theory of production--that production comes from mixing together land, labor, and capital and out comes potatoes or automobiles--is a preposterous oversimplification. Production functions are almost as worthless as the alchemists' attempts to transmute elements. Production, whether of biological organisms or of human artifacts, always begins with know-how--that is, the genetic factor. There were no plastics a hundred years ago because we did not know how to make them. Similarly, there were no human beings ten million years ago because the genetic structure of the earth did not know how to make us. There are no dinosaurs today because the biogenetic structure has forgotten how to make them.

This genetic structure, however, if it is to fulfill its potential and make what it knows how to make, must be able to capture energy to transport and to transform selected materials into the structures of the product. Energy of many different kinds and materials of many different kinds are the limiting factors in production. If we had no iron, we could not make steel even if we knew how to do it. If we did not have enough energy, we could not make steel either. Other limiting factors are space and time, for things occupy space and they take time to make. Here economics creeps in, economics being the study of scarcity. Being so obsessed by the cookbook theory, we have paid far too little attention to how the limiting factors actually limit production.

The genetic factor, what Julian Simon calls the "ultimate resource," has a profoundly uneconomic aspect to it, though it too undoubtedly has limits. The most important characteristic of information, even going back to bits and its successor concepts, is that it is not conserved. Even before life, chemical evolution was developing increasing complexity of molecular structures. With DNA, the information age really begins, for this is a structure capable of self-reproduction. Genetic know-how is fantastically multiplied in the organism itself as cells divide and as DNA reproduces itself. Similarly, know-what can be transmitted from one generation to the next by a learning process. When a good teacher teaches a class, at the end the class knows more and so does the teacher. The teacher does not lose what the class gains; there is no conservation.

Traditional economics has a kind of conservationist bias, as we see it in the extraordinary persistence of the illusion of economic equilibrium. The real world, however, has been a disequilibrium system from the "big bang" on. Evolution involves a constant disequilibrium, constant change. Adam Smith actually perceived this. He saw very clearly that it is knowledge that produces products, and that this has an enormous capacity for expansion, which is precisely what economic development consists in. This ultimate resource, because of its extraordinary power of self-multiplication, continually pushes back the limits of the limiting factors. The ultimate resource itself presumably has some ultimate limits, but we are certainly a very long way from them and do not know what they are.

In this sense, information economics symbolizes a return to some very profound insights that were there two hundred years ago, but which have been largely forgotten in the passion for equilibrium and quantification. We must be very careful, however, not to confuse information (in the information theory sense) with knowledge, either in the form of know-how, know-what, or know-whether. In many respects, information is the enemy of knowledge. Knowledge is often gained by the orderly loss of information and by restructuring it, filtering it. Piling information on information merely produces noise. Information is not simply "traded." In fact, the whole question as to what constitutes property in information and in knowledge is an extraordinarily tricky one and still needs a great deal more work done on it. Nevertheless, if we think of information economics as expanding to the study of know-how, know-what, and know-whether, it certainly has a very large and significant field to expand into.

COMMUNICATION AND INFORMATION ECONOMICS:
New Perspectives
M. Jussawalla and H. Ebenfield (Editors)

INTRODUCTION

It was not until 1976 that the American Economic Association added "information" to its classification 026, which previously covered "economics of uncertainty." The challenge of rapidly changing information technology to information theory and its application had been neglected by economists until it became impossible to ignore such areas as "informationally efficient markets" (Grossman and Stiglitz 1980) and the fact that economics of information is "intertwined with the most fundamental questions of economic organization" (Arrow 1980, 316). Lamberton (1980) has declared that the price system itself was an information system. The contributions of F.A. von Hayek, Herbert Simon, and Fritz Machlup added to the burgeoning literature on information economics (reviewed in an annotated bibliography by Middleton and Jussawalla 1981).

The traditional assumptions of economic theory are unable to accommodate the ramifications of the growing information-intensive economies of today. A new model of optimal resource allocation is needed that will account for the informational characteristics of a given economic problem. Is information a marketable commodity? Is it a resource that significantly alters the production function? How do instant communications via satellite and their interface with computers affect the micro foundations of economic behavior? There are both national and international dimensions to the economic problems raised by the workings of an information society.

At the December 1982 annual meeting of the American Economic Association two separate sessions were devoted to information/communication economics. Meheroo Jussawalla brought together a session on communication economics and development, under the chairmanship of Kenneth Boulding of the University of Colorado, and Helene Ebenfield arranged a session on the economics of information, under the chairmanship of Leonid Hurwicz of the University of Minnesota. The seven papers from these two sessions are presented in this volume in a collected fashion because all focus on various aspects of the emerging information sector and its bearing on growth, productivity investment, trade, and internal organization. The authors of the papers have all done research in diverse aspects of the subject, and their papers give the reader fresh perspectives on the dynamics of communication and information technology, as well as the implications for economic theory and its applications. Most of the papers point to the need for further empirical research, particularly in the field of productivity growth.

Lamberton in his paper has traced the historical development of information economics and its growing legitimacy as an area for future focus for economists. He finds that the scope of information economics is changing and becoming wider than earlier works in the area would suggest. He ascribes this trend to the growing importance of information with regard to productivity, competitive ability, and organizational structure. When combined with the implications of relaxing the "perfect competition" assumption of neoclassical and general equilibrium economics, there comes about a greater recognition of the widening scope of information economics. While he regards his literature review as highly selective, Lamberton has incorporated most of the relevant lines of research in historical perspective.

The importance of organizational change at all levels (firm, industry, nation, and world), how that change comes about, and the role of information within that change are then brought together in explaining the significance of investment. He analyzes the concept of investment in the bearing of past events on present decisions that influence organizational structures. Lamberton claims that just as past trends are important in assessing and understanding organizational changes, so also are they important for understanding the emergence of information economics.

This approach is further elaborated by Langlois in his analysis of internal organization and its theoretical implications. He demonstrates that the integration of an evolutionary or process view of economic change with the current transactions-cost approach towards the theory of internal organization may lead to a new conception of the term "efficiency" as it relates to an explanation of organizational form. Langlois argues that there is a distinction between structural and parametric knowledge and that the transactions-cost approach can be reduced analytically to the concept of imperfect structural knowledge. He then goes on to state that this conceptual base indicated a reinterpretation of efficiency explanations of internal organization.

This argument is developed through an examination of various earlier attempts to explain organizational behavior. The author notes that there are deficiencies in these explanations, especially as they relate to efficiency as the source of organizational form. Problems arise in two areas, viz disequilibria and path-dependency. While an organizational form may be efficient in some sense at a time when structural knowledge is relatively stable, it may not be once the equilibrium is disturbed. The path of adjustment between various equilibria also may be altered if the level of structural knowledge is changing. He finds that these considerations are of greater importance for understanding the origins of organizational behavior than for understanding the maintenance of either the internal or the market contract institutional forces. The paper closes with the suggestion that this area will prove fruitful for further empirical and historical research.

Organizational changes at the international level in dealing with information flows and trade in communications, along with their welfare implications, are dealt with by Jussawalla and Cheah. The authors examine information flows as being integral to international trade, its terms, and its composition and analyze the impact of such flows on trade theory and economic welfare. Trade in information, they assert, is germane to commerce, technology transfer, and national security. Jussawalla and Cheah discuss the less familiar economic issues of information flows and conceptualize these flows across national orders as an issue for the theory of international trade. The technology gap theory is then used to introduce a model for transborder data flows. Any improvement in innovative technology for information storage and retrieval will have a trade-increasing effect, if it reduces the cost of international communication. It is equally possible, however, for communication technology to create a trade-limiting effect by generating protectionist policies for safeguarding profits from innovative technology. Extending this argument to developing countries, the authors emphasize the role of transnational corporations in replacing the market in trade in information and in operating nonmarket systems for exports.

In an analysis of research and development, information, and productivity growth, Baumol and Wolff examine the seemingly inconsistent concurrence, in recent years, of an increase in the share of U.S. GNP being devoted to R&D with a decrease in the number of scientists and engineers employed. Another inconsistency noted by the authors is that while the ratio of outputs of the service and manufacturing sectors has remained fairly steady, labor employed by the services sector has grown. They contend that these two occurrences are related, and they have developed a model to explain these trends. It is based on Baumol's cost-disease model. The basic argument is that when there are differing rates of growth between two and later three sectors of their model, then the long-run result of interaction is that the rate of growth of the relatively stagnant sector acts as a brake on the overall rate of growth. This trend limits the influence of the more progressive sector in its effect on growth. They observe that the R&D sector may be an asymptotically stagnant sector, which explains the seeming inconsistencies with which the paper began. The authors make it specifically known that the outlays on R&D and the rate of growth of productivity can and must be determined simultaneously because of their endogenous nature.

A similar theme of productivity and growth for an information-intensive economy is dealt with by Jonscher. He substantiates the concept of an information sector and supports the validity of economic analysis that includes such a concept. He further stresses the importance of testing this approach through the development of theoretical models and subsequent testing of such models. Jonscher finds that development in the area of information-productivity relationships has, in the past, been "concerned with the analysis of information about some quite specific parameter of interest to our agent." He feels that a more generalized approach to the area is required to understand the broader trends and interactions of information sector growth and its bearing on productivity. The author presents his own efforts and results qualified by the belief that more research is required in this area.

The effects of technological change on the information sector are examined by Pulley and Braunstein. Their project builds upon earlier research done by Baumol, Braunstein, and others and also carries forward Jonscher's analysis by their emphasis on the scale augmenting implications of the impact of information technologies on the level of productivity. The authors estimate the extent of these scale and scope effects through an estimation of the cost function of a publisher of journals both before and after introducing an advanced information technology into that cost function. Their results show that there is a significant level of scale economies involved along with levels of scope economies and product-specific returns to scale. They assert that there is reason to associate these economies of scale and scope with the introduction of new technology. They find evidence of overall average incremental costs being reduced with the introduction of information technology. An important feature of their results is the use of firm-specific data to shape their estimation procedure in addition to the scale and scope effects of technology.

A useful growth model of the U.S. communications industry is described by Terleckyj, who provides a systematic analysis of the factors affecting the growth of the communications sector in the postwar period. The theoretical formulation of his model is based on previous research in the fields of research-and-development economics and productivity change. As such, his model (and the variations on it) includes the role of government expenditure on R&D and its effect on inducing private industry expenditure, the general level of economic activity, the R&D capital stock, and the price of communication output. Terleckyj's study shows that there is a significant relationship between government R&D expenditure and the level of private and total investment in communication during the first half of the period under study, 1948-1980. Communication output is found to depend on both the level of R&D capital and the level of total fixed capital. The price of communication output depends on the relative unit input in communication (which is the inverse to total factor productivity). The demand for communication output is considered to be a function of its relative price and the size of the economy, particularly during the second half of the period under study. The author concludes that further research is needed to establish the links between the growth of the communications sector and the the growth of productivity in the overall economy.

The editors arranged the sessions from which these papers emanated because of their interest in and conviction that information/communication economics is becoming increasingly important to economists, information scientists, managers, and others. Jussawalla has been doing research on information and communication economics at the East-West Center and is a frequent author and participant at conferences held throughout the world. Ebenfield spent many years as a program manager in the economics-of-information activity of the National Science Foundation (NSF) Division of Information Science and Technology and invited NSF grantees whose research would not only be of interest to attendees but also would highlight the wide range of interests of the Division of Science and Technology.

The editors are particularly grateful to the researchers who have contributed their papers to this volume and hope that readers will find interesting insights and new perspectives in the study of information/communication economics and its growing impact on economic development.

The editors also wish to acknowledge the editorial assistance of Michael E. Macmillan of the East-West Center Publications Office and to thank Joyce M. Gruhn and Michelle Rousseau of the East-West Center Institute of Culture and Communication, who typed the manuscript for publication. The support of the director of the Institute of Culture and Communication, Dr. Mary Bitterman, is also gratefully acknowledged.

REFERENCES

1 Arrow, K., The economics of information, in: Dertouzos, J., and Moses, J. (eds.), The Computer Age (MIT Press, Cambridge, Mass., 1980).

2 Grossman, S. and Stiglitz, J., On the impossibility of informationally efficient markets, American Economic Review 70, 3 (June 1980) 393-408.

3 Lamberton, D.M., Communication as a Discipline, paper presented at the ANZAAS Jublilee Conference, Adelaide (May 1980).

4 Middleton, K. and Jussawalla, M., Economics of Communication: An Annotated Bibliography with Abstracts (Pergamon Press, New York, 1981).

COMMUNICATION AND INFORMATION ECONOMICS:
New Perspectives
M. Jussawalla and H. Ebenfield (Editors)

THE EMERGENCE OF INFORMATION ECONOMICS

D. M. Lamberton

The emergence of information economics can be seen as a response to the deficiencies of economic theory built upon perfect knowledge, the failures of policy, or the spectacular advent of intelligent electronics with greatly enhanced capacity for communication, computation, and control. Whichever is the preferred interpretation, it remains a personal judgment whether the battle for recognition and respectability has only just been joined, is well advanced, has been won, or perhaps been lost.

There are numerous milestones. In 1976 the words "and information" were added to the entry "Economics of uncertainty" in the AEA Index of Economic Journals. Pioneering contributions, both theoretical and empirical, have been made over the last half century and more by, for example, Knight, Hayek, Jacob Marschak, Daniel Bell, Machlup, Shackle, Boulding, Kornai, Simon, and Arrow. More recently there have been surveys, e.g., by Spence (1974), Tomasini (1974), Lamberton (1971, 1974a, 1975, 1978, 1982), Hirshleifer and Riley (1979), and symposia and conferences, e.g., American Economic Association (1965), Princeton (1973), Lund (1974), Bell Journal (1975), International Economic Association (1975), Stanford (1975), City University of New York (1976), Unesco (1976), and IBM (1980). There is a burgeoning literature that reaches to every category of the AEA classification.[1] Some, for example Porat (1977), Sowell (1980), McCall (1982), Mackay (1982), and Nelson and Winter (1982), defy such processing while many address specific topics. All represent a challenge to orthodoxy. The tedious bibliographic detail serves to emphasize the pervasiveness of that challenge, to which might be added another: information economics is both bringing a new dimension to old interdisciplinary associations, as between economics and law, and creating new interdisciplinary links, as between economics and information science. To the extent that this spurs new territorial ambitions on the part of economists, they should perhaps reflect on motivation. Is it "that economists are looking for fields in which they can have some success" (Coase 1977, 484) or is there a growing realization that the role of information may be the key to real advancement of understanding economic phenomena?

Informational efficiency has been identified as a policy objective, and information resource management is seen as a method of achieving other policy objectives. Much of the modern thrust for this development came from the science sector, which all too often failed to appreciate that STI was only one of many information inputs (Lamberton 1976; Macdonald et al., forthcoming). The wisdom of the Piganiol O.E.C.D. Ad Hoc Group on Scientific and Technical Information has not always been heeded. Their report took the viewpoint of information specialists but added that "the Group has consistently tried to identify the way in which the 'information system' articulates with the structures of economic growth and, more broadly still, with the nature of political decisions" (O.E.C.D. 1971, 13). The policy debate has spread far beyond the O.E.C.D. In UN agencies, and Unesco in particular, the New International Information Order has been debated hotly. The policy needs for transition to the information society continue to be explored (NCLIS 1976; Dunn 1982; Bjørn-Anderson 1982).

As to the scope of national information policy, Dunn advocates boundaries that include "What we know as a people, what we are doing to learn more, and the tools that we use to conduct individual transactions and to communicate on a person-to-person basis." He argues that "There is a value in bringing together the ideas and issues involved in this set of national activities, because doing so calls to our attention the interrelatedness and importance in our lives. There are opportunities for improving the operation of the systems that provide information services. . . . Many of these opportunities will be enhanced by taking an integrated view of this area" (p. 38). The Japanese Fifth Generation Computer Project seeks to implement such an integrated view. Information processing systems are expected to play the following roles: (1) to increase productivity in low-productivity areas, (2) to meet international competition and contribute towards international cooperation, (3) to assist saving energy and resources, and (4) to cope with an aged society (JIPDEC 1981, 86).

If a copious literature and admission to the policy arena are not sufficient evidence of the emergence of information economics, it might be contended that it has a history.[2] Robbins (1968) is one of few to consider the longer history of the treatment of the advancement of knowledge in economic thought. He concedes "the neglect of knowledge" (Cannan 1929, 122-25) "as regards emphasis in the formal structure" but feels "that the picture is somewhat one-sided. It is just not true that the economic thought of the past was unaware of the relevance to development of technical or other forms of knowledge or that there is lacking in the literature conspicuous emphasis on its importance" (p. 83). He looks to the writings of Bentham, Babbage, Charles Knight, Rae, William Ellis, Harriet Martineau, the Millses, McCulloch, Senior, and Marshall. He might well have added Dugald Stewart (see Lamberton 1974b) and Thomas Hodgskin, chapter II of the latter's Popular Political Economy (1827) beginning "Influence of knowledge not noticed by economists till very lately" (p. 53).

Recognition of the importance of knowledge is only a first step toward an information economics. Early writers appear not to have gone very far in attempting to treat changes in knowledge as endogenous, although Williams's suggestion (1964, 174) that this began with Machlup must be questioned. Knight (1921) gave careful consideration to methods of meeting uncertainty. He observed that "information was one of the principal commodities" (p. 261) and that "vast sums of public money," "[g]reat investments of capital and elaborate organizations" were devoted to information activities. Admittedly he thought that they called for discussion, in the context of Risk, Uncertainty and Profit, "only insofar as they affect the general outline of the social economic structure" (p. 260). He pointed to "the existence of highly specialized industry structures performing the functions of furnishing knowledge and guidance" (p. 260). (Perhaps his comments did not attract as much attention as those of Machlup because he made no specific mention of the academic role!) Neither early writers nor Knight gave attention to the communication processes that were involved. Even into modern times communication concepts have remained primitive (Welch 1980), two fundamentally different concepts being distinguished: vertical between individual actors and a central agent and horizontal between actors.

Before pursuing Knight's question about the way in which methods of dealing with uncertainty affect "the general outline of the social economic structure," some consideration of definition is called for. Spence (1974) contended that recent interest in, for example, computers and telecommunications had obscured both "the pervasive influence of information in many other markets" and "the impact of the information sectors on the rest of the economy" (p. 57). This was being redressed by recent research which focused "largely upon the informational structure of markets" (p. 58).

Stiglitz (1977) in his introductory remarks to the Stanford symposium again emphasized the market context but took the view that imperfect information altered "the conventional notion of a market" (p. 389). Central statements from competitive theory became questionable. "The basic character of how we ought to view the competitive economy is altered if we take seriously imperfections of information" (p. 389). All papers in the symposium related to "the problems arising from costly information" (p. 389).

Hirshleifer and Riley (1979) drew a distinction between the economics of uncertainty where individuals are limited "to terminal actions, permitting them only to adapt to uncertainty" and the economics of information which examines "the consequences of informational actions, which allow [individuals] to overcome uncertainty" (p. 1393). Their survey captured a wide range of information activities: acquisition, dissemination, R&D, espionage and monitoring, wagering and speculation, signaling, and education, ending with comments on rational expectations and informational efficiency. Institutional aspects barely rated a mention. There are "interesting complications . . . when the informational decision process has multipersonal aspects" (p. 1397), but these were not pursued. Justifications for limiting property rights in ideas were admitted (p. 1405). It is concluded that "Information generation is in large part a disequilibrium-creating process, and information dissemination a disequilibrium-repairing process" (p. 1414). Where does organizational change of the kind plainly envisaged by Knight allow individuals to overcome uncertainty?

Arrow (1974, 1979) adds this new dimension. The last three decades have been preoccupied with decision making under a given uncertainty. "The problems of the economics of information proper arise when the probability distribution of states of the world is a variable" (1979, 308). This opens up ways of improving decision making. First, the decision maker can take advantage of the existence of signals. Secondly, the choice of which signals to receive becomes a decision variable. Thirdly, in sharp contrast to the individual decision maker who dominates the economics of information literature reviewed by Hirshleifer and Riley, a group or organization will normally be the real world decision maker. This is because, as Arrow says, "Specialization in information gathering is one instance, in [his] view the most important instance, of the economic benefits of organization" (1979, 310). To the extent that organizational structure and efficiency are not constrained fully by past events, organizational change becomes a third strategy for overcoming uncertainty and at the same time improves the prospects of the other two ways. Larger resources make possible fuller exploitation of the existence of signals while organizational capacity can widen the range of signals considered for reception. However, organizational structure may be inappropriate, and "Sclerosis of organizations may be as dangerous to health as sclerosis of the arteries" (Arrow 1979, 310). Arrow argues "that the combination of uncertainty, indivisibility, and capital intensity associated with information channels and their use imply (a) that the actual structure and behavior of an organization may depend heavily upon random events, in other words on history, and (b) the very pursuit of efficiency may lead to rigidity and unresponsiveness to further change" (1974, 49).

There would appear to be major implications for economic theory. The Hayekian approach, which emphasized that the economy was an information system but held that there were important limitations on the availability of information, left the institutional structure intact, with the consequence--for the most part not mentioned--of probable advantage to those individuals and organizations "having access to better information, or a better position in the institutional structure" (Starrett 1976, 282). This is equally true of the original version, the modernization by Sowell, or the resurrection by the rational (consistent) expectations approach as reviewed, for example, by Begg (1982). This latter approach prompted the comment that "It would be ironic if the outcome of a decade and a half of concern with the economics of (imperfect) knowledge resulted in the renewed dominance of models incorporating perfect knowledge assumptions" (O'Driscoll 1979, 157). The biggest loss might well prove to be the inhibiting of the attempt by economists to probe deeply into the organizational aspects of the economy.

Of course, it might be argued that economics, in order to cope with disequilibria, is devoting more attention to how decisions are made. Various approaches to procedural rationality have been developed: OR and management science, artificial intelligence, computational complexity, and cognitive simulation (Simon 1978). These approaches appear to be concerned with "the distinction between the perceived environment and the environment" (Hahn 1973, 40), or, as Simon put it, "procedural rationality is the rationality of a person for whom computation is the scarce resource" (1978, 504). He argues that there is no theorem that proves the process will converge to limit survival to those who have found the objective optimum: "It is much more likely, in a world with rapidly advancing human knowledge and technology, with an unpredictable shifting political situation, with recurrent and unforeseen (if not always unforeseeable) impacts of demographic, environmental, and other changes, that the location of the objective optimum has little relevance for the decision makers or the situations that their decisions create" (1978, 505).

procedural rationality ⇓ A.I, cognitive simulation

Simon believes normative microeconomics, the theory of the business cycle, and the Schumpeterian domain of long-term dynamics are specific domains that can benefit from the procedural rationality approach. This may be beyond challenge, but some queries do arise. Consider the long term. Here the contention is that "The search for new products or new marketing strategies surely resembles the search for a good chess move more than it resembles the search for a hilltop" (Simon 1978, 505). Even if this is correct, it remains possible that the decision strategy bears little resemblance to the search for a good chess move once it is recognized that the strategy can take advantage of the existence of signals, that the choice of signals to receive has to be made, and that the organization itself is a variable.

The study of organizational change and organizational options should then be properly an activity for economists. Comments and efforts here are of various kinds. For example, in the context of industrial economics Bradburd and Over (1982) treat an industry's monopoly price as a "collective good" achieved and sustained by organizing. "The costs of the necessary organization can be divided into those incurred in the formation of the organization and those incurred in maintaining it. In order to establish the communication demands, signaling mechanisms, and other rules of behavior which govern the operation of an organized industry, and in order to determine initially how the costs and benefits of the collective good are to be apportioned, an industry must incur fixed formation costs. . . . Maintaining the organization to ensure adherence to the price and output policies agreed to when the organization was formed is also costly. Resources must be expended to maintain channels of communication and on other interfirm activities such as exchanging information and policing the industry agreement, as well as on all intrafirm communication that guides the marketing department in its efforts to compete vigorously without violating the industry agreement" (p. 51). The existence of organizational capital leads to separate integrative and disintegrative levels of concentration. Teubal (forthcoming) likewise assigns an important role to "intangibles accumulation or capability creation, of which knowledge from R&D is just one possibility." Both those efforts are in the tradition of the pioneering work of P.W.S. Andrews (1949), who distinguished between technical and managerial costs and examined the effects of changing organization (ch. iv).

At the international level, supranational forms of organization have received too little attention from economists: one must turn to journals of international business and even anthropology (e.g., Wolfe 1977). While transborder data flow studies have tended to emphasize an underlying free trade vs. dependence conflict, they also have begun to cast new light on specialization in and location of the activities of multinationals. Two intriguing aspects of current developments in communications technology might be noted. These developments challenge the new orthodoxy according to which "technology . . . has never been so internationally mobile. It now seems that only labor is a geographically fixed factor" (Stout 1980, 165). In some ways these international firms might be viewed as organizations for international cooperation which then brings them within the scope of efforts to compare the efficiency of alternative forms (e.g., Tinbergen 1978).

These few samples of recent research initiatives illustrate the potential importance of organizational change at the level of the firm,[3] the industry, nationally, and globally. The terminology differs: organizational capital, information stock, capability, intangibles.[4] In each case a form of investment is involved: investment that allows for the influence of past events on present decisions.

How does organizational change come about? What is the role of information in that process? One response can be to proceed as has commonly been done with technology: to assume that there is an organization manual and that an optimal choice of organizational form will be made from the large number of alternatives listed. However, this makes no more sense for choice of organization than for choice of technology (cf. Nelson 1980). The pages of such a manual are widely scattered, are costly to locate and translate, and have very limited application to the special circumstances of the existing organization, constrained as it is by its organizational assets.

Schotter's (1982) attempt to provide an economic theory of social institutions may in due course help in answering this question. Institutions are regarded as regularities in the behavior of social agents. These regularities, created by the agents themselves, are used as informational devices to supplement competitive price information. So his attempt shares the interest of this chapter in the analysis of organizational forms. It does, however, suffer from a limitation that has been noted in other contexts--it is basically concerned with dynamic adjustments to a static state of nature (cf. Slater 1982, 715). Can analysis be widened to deal with situations in which the strategies and payoffs are shaped by the form of organization? It should be noted also that Schotter's work "is not a contribution to public choice theory" (Slater 1982, 714). While it is true that Schotter is concerned with sets of rules agreed on by individuals, his analysis might well illuminate circumstances and processes that could be ignored by public decision makers at their peril when they see fit to impose sets of rules that have not been agreed on.

All these matters might perhaps continue to be neglected if information and organization costs were minor. However, the use of a revised national accounting approach, supplemented by occupational classifications, has tended to confirm the increasing information intensity of economic systems. A recent O.E.C.D. publication (1981) is a convenient way of summarizing this approach and its results. Table 1 and Fig. 1 show that all the countries covered have undergone a profound change in their occupational structure, the share of information occupations in the economically active increasing by about 3 percent in each five-year period. Such occupations account for more than one-third of the labor force in these countries. About two in every three people in these occupations were engaged in routine information handling activities.

There are no doubt many problems in the collection of such statistics. Nevertheless, their analysis has involved several established dichotomies: information vs. non-information; information investment vs. information consumption; routine vs. non-routine information activities (O.E.C.D. 1981). The question to be raised here is whether that approach can incorporate a treatment of organizational change. It is possible, for example, to separate out the creation of new knowledge and then treat the balance of information activity as organizational--as the cost of running the system. This procedure has several deficiencies.

If R&D as now conventionally measured is taken as the expenditure on new knowledge creation, the net is too narrow in that this scientist's definition of R&D excludes a significant part of innovation costs that could properly be held to create knowledge. At the same time, much expenditure that is little more than the maintenance of stocks of knowledge and manpower will be included. More significantly in the present context, the residual information expenditures after the exclusion of R&D will include expenditures both to create and to maintain organizational capital. These dividing lines are blurred by the difficulties of giving precise meanings to the obsolescence of information and organizational capacity.

The possibilities of using the distinction between production and organization, the latter being equated with an adjusted information sector, have been touched on by Jonscher (1982). Of course, it is easy to overlook the possibility that expenditures fail to achieve the objectives that led to their being incurred. Because information technologies seem so difficult to evaluate, this form of failure has been labeled "the Xerox effect" (Lamberton et al. 1982). The further possibility that activities included

Table 1

Typology of Information Occupations

INFORMATION PRODUCERS:	Scientific and technical workers (components); market search and coordination specialists; information gatherers; consultative services.
INFORMATION PROCESSORS:	Administrative and managerial; process control and supervisory; clerical and related (components).
INFORMATION DISTRIBUTORS:	Educators; communication workers.
INFORMATION INFRASTRUCTURE OCCUPATIONS:	Information machine workers; postal and telecommunications.

INFORMATION PRODUCERS create new information or package existing information into a form appropriate to a particular recipient. Scientific and technical workers primarily engage in research, development, and other inventive activities. Information gatherers include various occupations that, by investigation and assessment, are mainly concerned with creating new information. Market search and coordination specialists provide, via search activities, market information to buyers, sellers, or both. Consultative services primarily apply a pre-existent body of information to the particular needs of the client or situation.

INFORMATION PROCESSORS are primarily concerned with receiving and responding to information inputs. The response may be to decide, to administer, or to perform some manipulative operation upon the information inputs. Administrative and managerial occupations receive information in the form of details about firm (or departmental) performance and environment, instructions from above, etc., all of which are processed into some form of communication to those superior or subordinate to them. Their job is to decide, organize, plan, interpret, or execute policy, whether in private or public undertakings. Process control and supervisory occupations also coordinate and control, though usually in the more specific context of a particular technical process or body of subordinate workers engaged in such a process. Clerical and related occupations receive information as correspondence and data, verbal or recorded, and manipulate such inputs into a form appropriate to the employer.

INFORMATION DISTRIBUTORS are primarily concerned with conveying information from the initiator to the recipient. Educators mainly convey information that has already been produced. Communication workers include various occupations in the news and entertainment media. Both groups include elements of information production (e.g., research activities of university teachers and investigative journalism), but the primary activity is considered distributive.

INFORMATION INFRASTRUCTURE occupations install, operate, and repair machines and technologies used to support information activities.

Source: Adapted from O.E.C.D. 1981, Vol. 1, p. 24.

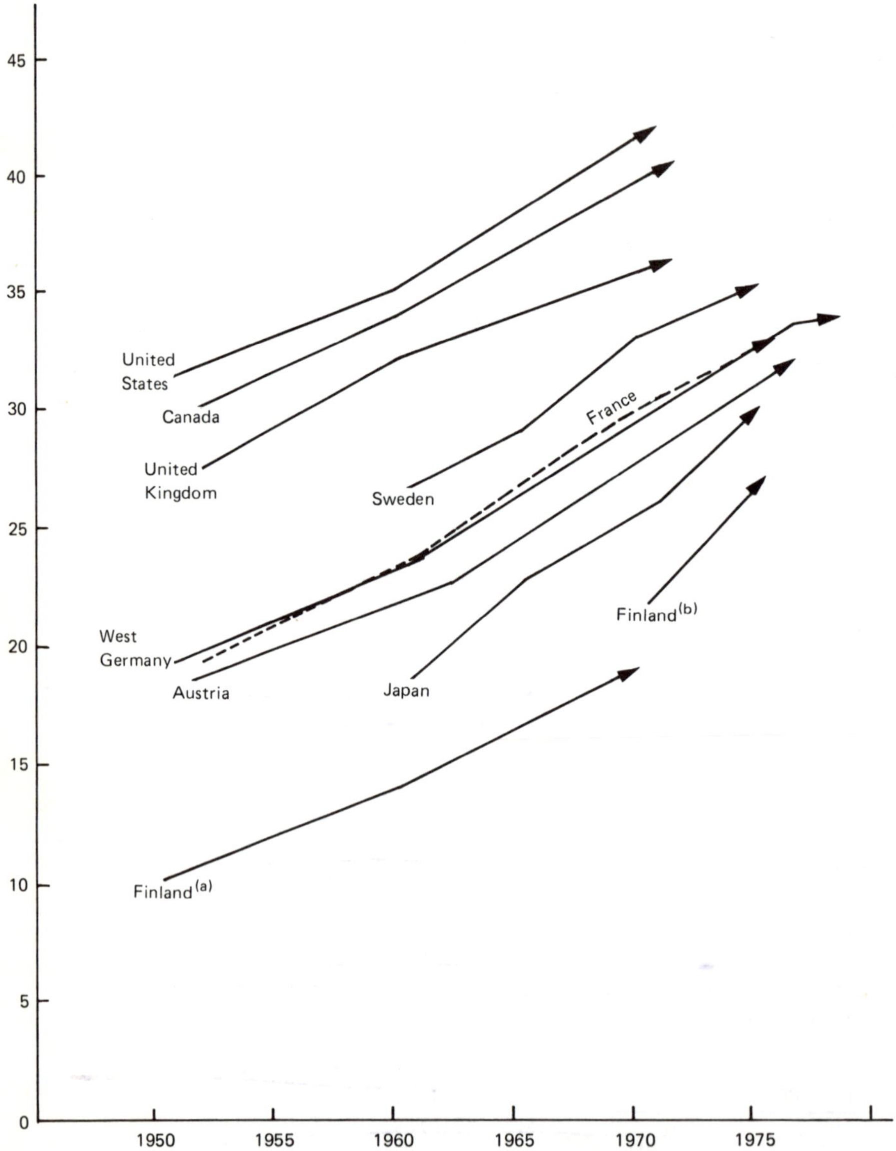

Source: O.E.C.D. 1981, vol. 1, p. 25.

Data for Finland were derived from two separate sources: (a) Pietarinen and (b) The Central Statistical Office of Finland, both sources using a rather more restricted definition of information occupations than other countries. Absolute values for any given year are, therefore, not strictly comparable with other countries, although the trend is still of interest.

Fig. 1. Information occupations as a percentage of economically active

in the information sector may be unproductive is emphasized by Bhagwati (1982): for example, lobbying for protection, competing for a share of licenses, evading governmental regulations. It should, however, be noted that these activities may draw upon the same organizational capacities as other activities deemed of social value in a dynamic context, for example, for innovation.

In 1972 Arrow was reported (New York Times) as viewing information economics "as an effort to plug a hole" in the theory of general equilibrium. Even if no more than this be involved, his position represented a big advance on the view that information could be treated as just one more commodity. (Perhaps some of the inadequacies of this view can be probed by considering what is implied if a perfect holiday or perfect transport or perfect manufactured goods were assumed!) Simon has pointed out that there are "some standard techniques for avoiding a separate theory of procedural rationality--in particular the proposal that we simply fold in the costs of computation with all of the other costs in the general optimization problem" (1978, 506). He believed that this would leave "unanswered all of the fascinating and important questions of what constitutes an efficient decision-making procedure" (p. 506). This chapter is in agreement. It has endeavored to interpret the emergence of information economics, to provide a highly selective guide to some of its literature, and to comment upon significant research directions. Perhaps echoing Chamberlin's well-known paper, an alternative title would have been "The Organization as a Variable." Economists may have to draw upon organizational science (e.g., Ramos 1981) and information science in this effort, but history (e.g., Chandler 1977; Williamson 1981) will be a necessary companion discipline.[5]

NOTES

1 The following are illustrative: 000--Grossman and Stiglitz, "On the Impossibility of Informationally Efficient Markets;" Welch, "Vertical and Horizontal Communication in Economic Processes;" 100--Jussawalla and Lamberton (eds.), Communication Economics and Development; Gertler, "Imperfect Information and Wage Inertia in the Business Cycle;" 200--O.E.C.D., Information Activities, Electronics and Telecommunication Technologies Impact on Employment Growth and Trade; Jussawalla and Cheah, Towards an Information Economy: A Case Study of Singapore (mimeo); 300--Mansfield, "Tax Policy and Innovation;" Pommerehne and Schneider, "Fiscal Illusion, Political Institutions, and Local Public Spending;" 400--Caves et al., "The Imperfect Market for Technology Licenses;" NTIA, Trade Issues in Telecommunications and Information; 500--Hodgson and Eade, Information Systems in Public Administration; McMillan, "Robotics Will the Corporation be Managed by Machines?"; 600--Bradburd and Over, "Organizational Costs, Sticky Equilibria, and Critical Levels of Concentration;" Wigand, "The Communication Industry in Economic Integration: The Case of West Germany;" 700--Riemenschneider and Bonnen, "National Agricultural Information Systems: Design and Assessment;" Crouch and Chamala, Extension Education and Rural Development; 800--Backhouse, Information Services for Trade Unionists; Mauro, "Strikes as a Result of Imperfect Information;" 900--Beales et al., "The Efficient Regulation of Consumer Information;" Schuman, "Information Justice."

2 Some might say that the final badge is having its own journal, the publication of Information Economics and Policy having been announced last year by North-Holland Publishing Company. While such a publication fits the general pattern of increasing specialization in information activities, one might have mixed feelings because some colleagues are inclined to interpret information economics as just another field of specialization rather than an attempt to address the really big problems of economics.

3 "For the study of the individual firm it must be recognized that the firm possesses a stock of capital, an organization, and a stock of information which will be modified by the firm's own endeavors and not merely as an automatic result of the operation of the market" (Lamberton 1965, 7).

4 McCain's tradition comes close to Teubal's concept (1981).

5 Some interesting cases of and suggestions for organizational innovation might be Japan's MITI, "Commerce on the campus" (The Economist 1982b), a high-technology Morrill Act (Botkin et al. 1982), Los Angeles' Telacu and Uno ventures (The Economist 1982a), or Australia's Snowy Mountains Engineering Corporation (Price and Elston 1980).

REFERENCES

1 American Economic Association Conference [1965], American Economic Review 56, 2 (May 1966).

2 Andrews, P.W.S., Manufacturing Business (Macmillan, London, 1949).

3 Arrow, K.J., The Limits of Organization (Norton, New York, 1974).

4 Arrow, K.J., The economics of information, in: Dertouzos, M.L. and Moses, Joel (eds.), The Computer Age: A Twenty-Year View (MIT Press, Cambridge, 1979) 306-317.

5 Backhouse, R., Information Services for Trade Unionists (Elm Publications, London, 1982).

6 Beales, H., Craswell, R. and Salop, S.C., The efficient regulation of consumer information, Journal of Law and Economics XXIV (December 1981) 491-544.

7 Begg, D.K.H., The Rational Expectations Revolution in Macroeconomics Theories and Evidence (Philip Allan, Oxford, 1982).

8 Bell, D., The Coming of Post-Industrial Society (Basic Books, New York, 1973).

9 Bell, D., The information society, in: Dertouzos, M.L. and Moses, J. (eds.), The Computer Age: A Twenty-Year View, (MIT Press, Cambridge, 1979) 163-211.

10 Bell Journal Symposium on The Economics of Internal Organization, Bell Journal of Economics 6, 1 (Spring 1975).

11 Bhagwati, J.N., Directly unproductive, profit-seeking (DUP) activities, Journal of Political Economy 90, 5 (October 1982) 988-1002.

12 Bjørn-Anderson, N., Earl, M., Holst, O., and Mumford, E. (eds.) Information Society: For Richer, For Poorer, (North-Holland, Amsterdam, 1982).

13 Botkin, J., Dimancescu, D., and Stata, R., High technology, higher education, and high anxiety, Technology Review 85, 7 (October 1982) 49-57.

14 Boulding, K.E., The economics of knowledge and the knowledge of economics, American Economic Review 56, 2 (May 1966) 1-13 (Reprinted in Lamberton (ed.) 1971, 21-36).

15 Bradburd, R.M., and Over, Mead A., Jr., Organizational costs, sticky equilibria, and critical levels of concentration, Review of Economics and Statistics 64 (February 1982) 50-58.

16 Cannan, E., Review of Economic Theory (Frank Cass, London, 1929).

17 Caves, R.E., Crookell, H., and Killing, J.P., The Imperfect Market for Technology Licenses, Harvard Institute of Economic Research Discussion Paper No. 903 (June 1982).

18 Chandler, A.D., Jr., The Visible Hand: The Managerial Revolution in American Business (The Belknap Press of Harvard University Press, 1977).

19 City University of New York Conference on Economics of Information [1976], Galatin, M. and Leiter, R.D. (eds.), Economics of Information (Martinus Nijhoff, Boston, 1981).

20 Coase, R.H., Economics and Contiguous Disciplines, in: Perlman, M. (ed.), The Organization and Retrieval of Economic Knowledge (Macmillan, London, 1977) 481-495.

21 Crouch, B.R. and Chamala, S. (eds.), Extension Education and Rural Development Vol. 1, International Experience in Communication and Innovation (Wiley, New York, 1981).

22 Dunn, D.A., Developing information policy, Telecommunications Policy 6, 1 (March 1982) 21-38.

23 The Economist, American survey: Los Angeles (April 3, 1982a) 57-88.

24 The Economist, Commerce on the campus (January 23, 1982b) 76.

25 Gertler, M., Imperfect information and wage inertia in the business cycle, Journal of Political Economy 90, 5 (October 1982) 967-987.

26 Grossman, S.J. and Stiglitz, J.E., On the impossibility of informationally efficient markets, American Economic Review 70, 3 (June 1980) 393-408.

27 Hahn, F.H., On the Notion of Equilibrium in Economics (Cambridge University Press, Cambridge, 1973).

28 Hirshleifer, J. and Riley, J.G., The analytics of uncertainty and information--an expository survey, Journal of Economic Literature 17 (December 1979) 1375-1421.

29 Hodgskin, T., Popular Political Economy (Augustus M. Kelley, New York, 1827) (Reprints of Economic Classics 1966).

30 Hodgson, J. and Eade, D. (eds.), Information Systems in Public Administration (North-Holland, Amsterdam, 1982).

31 IBM Symposium on The Economics of Information Processing [1980], Goldberg, R. and Lorin, H. (eds.), The Economics of Information Processing 1-2, (Wiley-Interscience, New York, 1982).

32 International Economic Association Conference [1975], Perlman, M. (ed.), The Organization and Retrieval of Economic Knowledge (Macmillan, London, 1977).

33 JIPDEC (Japan Information Processing Development Center), Preliminary Report on Study and Research on Fifth-Generation Computers 1979-80 (1981).

34 Jonscher, C., Notes on Communication and Economic Theory, in: Jussawalla, M. and Lamberton, D.M. (eds.) (1982) 60-69.

35 Jussawalla, M. and Cheah, Chee-Wah (mimeo), Towards an Information Economy: A Case Study of Singapore (1982).

36 Jussawalla, M. and Lamberton, D.M. (eds.), Communication Economics and Development (Pergamon Press, New York, 1982).

37 Knight, F.H., Risk, Uncertainty, and Profit, (Houghton Mifflin, Boston, 1921).

38 Kornai, J., Anti-Equilibrium (North-Holland, Amsterdam, 1971).

39 Lamberton, D.M., The Theory of Profit (Basil Blackwell, Oxford, 1965).

40 Lamberton, D.M. (ed.), The Economics of Information and Knowledge (Penguin Books, Harmondsworth, 1971).

41 Lamberton, D.M. (ed.), The Information Revolution, The Annals of the American Academy of Political and Social Science 412 (March 1974a).

42 Lamberton, D.M., Dugald Stewart's Work on Technological Change (mimeo) (1974b).

43 Lamberton, D.M., Who Owns the Unexpected? (University of Queensland Press, St. Lucia, 1975).

44 Lamberton, D.M., National policy for economic information, International Social Science Journal 28, 3 (1976) 449-465.

45 Lamberton, D.M., The Economics of Communication, S. Rahim et al., Planning Methods, Models, and Organizations (East-West Communication Institute, Honolulu, 1978).

46 Lamberton, D.M., The Theoretical Implications of Measuring the Communication Sector, in: Jussawalla and Lamberton (eds.), 36-59.

47 Lamberton, D.M., Macdonald, S. and Mandeville, T.D., Productivity and technological change, Canberra Bulletin of Public Administration IX, 2 (Winter 1982) 23-30.

48 Lund Symposium on The Economics of Information, The Swedish Journal of Economics 76 (1974).

49 Macdonald, S., Lamberton, D.M. and Mandeville, T.D. (eds.), The Trouble with Technology (Frances Pinter, London; St. Martin's Press, New York, forthcoming).

50 Machlup, F., The Production and Distribution of Knowledge in the United States (Princeton University Press, Princeton, N.J., 1963).

51 Machlup, F., Knowledge: Its Creation, Distribution, and Economic Significance, Vol. 1: Knowledge and Knowledge Production (Princeton University Press, Princeton, N.J., 1980).

52 Machlup, F., Knowledge: Its Creation, Distribution, and Economic Significance, Vol. II: The Branches of Learning, Information Sciences, and Human Capital (Princeton University Press, Princeton, N.J., 1982).

53 Mackaay, E., Economics of Information and Law (Kluwer Boston, Hingham, 1982).

54 Mansfield, E., Tax policy and innovation, Science 215, 4538 (March 12, 1982) 1365-1371.

55 Marschak, J., Economic Information, Decision and Prediction Selected Essays: Vol. II Economics of Information and Organization (D. Reidel, Boston, 1974).

56 Mauro, M.J., Strikes as a result of imperfect information, Industrial and Labor Relations Review 35, 4 (July 1982) 522-538.

57 McCain, R.A., Tradition and Innovation: Some Economics of the Creative Arts, Science, Scholarship, and Technical Development, in: Galatin, M. and Leiter, R.D. (eds.), Economics of Information (Martinus Nijhoff, Boston, 1981) 173-208.

58 McCall, J.J. (ed.), The Economics of Information and Uncertainty (University of Chicago Press, Chicago, 1982).

59 McMillan, J., Robotics will the corporation be managed by machines?, Cost and Management 56, 4 (July-August 1982) 2-7.

60 NCLIS (National Commission on Libraries and Information Science), National Information Policy (U.S. Government Printing Office, Washington, 1976).

61 Nelson, R.R., Production sets, technological knowledge, and R & D: fragile and overworked constructs for analysis of productivity growth?, American Economic Review 70, 2 (May 1980) 62-67.

62 Nelson, R.R. and Winter, S.G., An Evolutionary Theory of Economic Change (Harvard University Press, 1982).

63 New York Times, Nobel Winner Engrossed by Balancing Act (November 26, F5, 1972).

64 NTIA (National Telecommunications and Information Administration), Trade Issues in Telecommunications and Information I-IV (U.S. Department of Commerce, Washington, 1981).

65 O'Driscoll, G.P., Jr., Rational Expectations, Politics, and Stagflation, in: Rizzo, M.J. (ed.), Time, Uncertainty and Disequilibrium (Lexington Books, Lexington, Mass., 1979) 153-176.

66 O.E.C.D., Information for a Changing Society. Some Policy Considerations, (O.E.C.D., Paris, 1971).

67 O.E.C.D., Information Activities, Electronics and Telecommunications Technologies Impact on Employment, Growth and Trade 1-11 (O.E.C.D., Paris, 1981).

68 Pommerehne, W.W. and Schneider, F., Fiscal illusion, political institutions, and local public spending, Kyklos 31, 3 (1978) 381-408.

69 Porat, M.U., The Information Economy 1-9 (Office of Telecommunications, U.S. Department of Commerce, Washington, 1977).

70 Price, D.G. and Elston, J.W., Developing Countries' Avenues for Assistance--Advantages and Disadvantages, First International Conference on Technology for Development 1980 (The Institution of Engineers, Canberra, 1980).

71 Princeton Symposium: The economics of information [1973], Quarterly Journal of Economics 90, 4 (November 1976).

72 Ramos, A.G., The New Science of Organizations: A Reconceptualization of the Wealth of Nations (University of Toronto Press, Toronto, 1981).

73 Riemenschneider, C.H. and Bonnen, J.T., National Agricultural Information Systems: Design and Assessment, in: Blackie, M.J. and Dent, J.B. (eds.), Information Systems for Agriculture (Applied Science Publishers, London, 1979).

74 Robbins, Lord, The Theory of Economic Development in the History of Economic Thought (Macmillan, London, 1968).

75 Schotter, A., The Economic Theory of Social Institutions (Cambridge University Press, Cambridge, 1981).

76 Schuman, P.G., Information justice, Library Journal 107, 11 (June 1, 1982) 1060-1066.

77 Shackle, G.L.S., Decision Order and Time in Human Affairs, 2nd edition (Cambridge University Press, Cambridge, 1969).

78 Simon, H.A., On how to decide what to do, Bell Journal of Economics 9, 2 (Autumn 1978) 494-507.

79 Slater, J.R., Review of Schotter, The economic theory of social institutions, Economic Journal 92, 367 (September 1982) 714-715.

80 Sowell, T., Knowledge and Decisions (Basic Books, New York, 1980).

81 Spence, A.M., An Economist's View of Information, in: Cuadra, C.A. and Luke, A.W. (eds.), Annual Review of Information Science and Technology 9 (American Society for Information Science, Washington, 1974).

82 Stanford Symposium on Economics of Information [1975], Review of Economic Studies 44 (1977) 389-599.

83 Starrett, D., Social institutions, imperfect information, and the distribution of income, Quarterly Journal of Economics 90, 2 (May 1976) 261-284.

84 Stiglitz, J.E., Symposium on economics of information: introduction, Review of Economic Studies 44 (1977) 389-391.

85 Stout, D.K., The impact of technology on economic growth in the 1980s, Daedalus (Winter 1980) 159-167.

86 Teubal, M., Some Notes on the Accumulation of Intangibles by High-Technology Firms, in: Macdonald, Lamberton and Mandeville (forthcoming).

87 Tinbergen, J., Alternative forms of international cooperation: comparing their efficiency, International Social Science Journal 30, 2 (1978) 223-237.

88 Tomasini, L.M., The economics of information: A survey, Economie Appliquee 27, 2-3 (1974) 319-337.

89 Unesco special issue on Economics of information and information for economists, International Social Science Journal 28, 3 (1976).

90 Von Hayek, F.A., Economics and knowledge, Economica, N.S. 4 (February 1937) 33-54.

91 Von Hayek, F.A., The pretence of knowledge, Swedish Journal of Economics 77, 4 (1975) 433-442.

92 Welch, R.L., Vertical and horizontal communication in economic processes, Review of Economic Studies 47 (1980) 733-746.

93 Wigand, R.T., The communication industry in economic integration: the case of West Germany, Social Networks 4, 1 (March 1982) 47-79.

94 Williams, B.R., Review of F. Machlup, The production and distribution of knowledge in the United States, Economic Journal LXXIV, 293 (March 1964) 174-175.

95 Williamson, O.E., The modern corporation: origins, evolution, attributes, Journal of Economic Literature 19, 4 (December 1981) 1537-1568.

96 Wolfe, A.W., The supranational organization of production: An evolutionary perspective, Current Anthropology 18, 4 (December 1977) 615-635.

COMMUNICATION AND INFORMATION ECONOMICS:
New Perspectives
M. Jussawalla and H. Ebenfield (Editors)

INTERNAL ORGANIZATION IN A DYNAMIC CONTEXT: SOME THEORETICAL CONSIDERATIONS

Richard N. Langlois

INTRODUCTION

This essay attempts to suggest how process or evolutionary considerations might best be integrated into the rapidly developing transaction-cost approach to the theory of internal organization. The analysis begins by arguing that the theoretical issues in the transaction-cost approach to organization reduce to and can be integrated around a single analytical concept: imperfect structural (as distinguished from parametric) knowledge. The paper goes on to argue that this concept points toward a reinterpretation of efficiency explanations of internal organization in terms of an evolutionary logic of explanation. The article concludes by showing how such a reinterpretation might proceed and suggests some substantive implications susceptible to empirical and historical scrutiny.

The last decade has seen a burgeoning of interest in the economics of internal organization.[1] This young area has already produced a literature rich in new understandings of the nature and function of nonmarket modes of organization--that is, of modes of economic coordination alternative to price-mediated spot transactions.

To a very great extent, the fruitfulness of this literature can be traced to a willingness to abandon, to one degree or another, the formulations of neoclassical welfare economics in favor of a comparative-institutional analysis along the lines pioneered by Ronald Coase (1937, 1960). Rather than proceeding from an axiomatic optimization-and-equilibrium framework in which all transactions are portrayed as costless and contemporaneous, this latter approach prefers explicitly to compare alternative organizational arrangements--what Williamson (1979) calls governance structures--according to the kinds and costs of transacting each involves.[2]

But the fruitfulness of the modern literature of internal organization has not itself been entirely costless. In deviating from the more conventional paths, the comparative-institutional approach gives up some of the tidiness and formal unity that an axiomatic-maximization framework has bestowed upon the Walrasian tradition.

The trade is still an extremely favorable one for the comparative-institutional approach. Some loss of formal elegance is arguably a small price to pay to improve upon a theory that, as is often remarked, not only leaves the existence of business firms entirely unexplained but actually analyzes a world in which such firms should not exist (Loasby 1976). The modern theory of internal organization, moreover, is certainly not without theoretical coherence; it may even be said to have a single unifying principle: the notion of the transaction cost. Nonetheless, there remains a sense in which the eclecticism of the comparative-institutional approach borders on the ad hoc; and, as even the most ardent proponents of this approach admit, the idea of a transaction cost is itself still a somewhat fuzzy concept (Williamson 1979).

Part of this untidy appearance is surely endemic to the nature of the phenomena under study; it cannot--and should not--be eliminated. There really is some trading off to be done between theoretical elegance and explanatory power. At the same time, I would argue, part of the seemingly ad hoc character of transaction-cost analysis is not entirely ineluctable and arises from a rather different source. In rejecting, whether implicitly or explicitly, the formal core of mainstream neoclassical theory, the internal organization literature has abandoned one organizing principle--one microeconomic logic--without having found another to take its place. It is a literature that employs many of the trappings of neoclassical theory (e.g., maximizing language and an apparent equilibrium orientation) to express insights that (as I shall argue) are fundamentally antagonistic to the neoclassical research program. Life in this sort of theoretical limbo is guaranteed to breed an appearance of being ad hoc.

Fortunately, there is, I believe, an alternate theoretical structure with which the transaction-cost approach might ally itself: the dynamic or evolutionary[3] view of economics. This essay attempts to suggest how such a connection might be made. I will argue (a) that the basic insight of the transaction-cost approach already implies an evolutionary view of economics; (b) that such a view helps reinterpret results from the theory of internal organization in a way that makes the analysis seem far less ad hoc; and (c) that a dynamic orientation has substantive implications for our understanding of organizational form that are not now fully recognized in the literature.

Transaction Costs and Internal Organization

It is not without justification that historical discussions of the theory of internal organization invariably point to Ronald Coase's 1937 article "The Nature of the Firm" as a (and sometimes the) seminal article in the field. But there is also an important sense in which a later article by Coase--one seemingly aimed at a quite different area of theory--has held equally important insights for the modern comparative-institutional analysis of organizations.

In the 1937 article, Coase took up a question that economists had, to that point, largely ignored.[4] Why is some economic activity organized within business firms? Why is not all economic activity coordinated by prices and markets? Coase's answer is that there is "a cost to using the price system" (Coase 1937, 390). The costs to which he points are clearly recognizable as the same sorts of transaction costs that animate present-day discussions.[5] But the Coase of 1937 was less interested in institutional comparisons than in reconciling analysis of the firm with the basic concepts of Marshallian comparative-statics. Thus the famous assertion that the firm will expand until the cost of internalizing the next transaction is equal to the cost of leaving that transaction to the price system (Coase 1937, 395).

It was really in Coase's 1960 article, "The Problem of Social Cost," that the importance and implications of transaction costs crystallized in clearly institutional form. The article is a reexamination of the problem of externalities or, more specifically, of incompatible uses of property rights. Coase attacks what he describes as the Pigouvian tradition, in which incompatible uses were understood in terms of a divergence between private and social cost caused by so-called physical externalities. And his method of attack is to effect what one might call an externality shift: in the absence of transaction costs, Coase argues, all incompatibilities in the use of property rights would be resolved in more-or-less optimal fashion; the problem, therefore, is not the physical externality at all but whatever informational or public-goods type externality lies behind the transaction costs that impede bargaining. The most important implication of this externality shift is a redirection of attention away from a market failure conception of the problem toward an analysis in which the properties--including transaction-cost properties--of alternative institutional arrangements are the principal focus (Dahlman 1979).

The modern literature of internal organization reflects, in effect, a recognition that this logic of analysis can be extended beyond the range of incompatible-use problems with which Coase was concerned in the 1960 article. In general, there are a number of arrangements one might consider as ways of resolving pollution or nuisance-type incompatibilities: contractual agreements, as between the farmer and the rancher in Coase's famous example, might be one way; rules and social conventions might be another; and the exchange of property rights--as when one owner buys out the other--might be a third way. But these alternatives do not present themselves only in response to physical externalities of the nuisance/pollution sort; they are quite general phenomena of production and economic exchange.

Among the many institutional comparisons to which the theorist of organizational form might address himself, perhaps the most intriguing is that between the system of coordinating economic activity through price-mediated spot-contract exchanges (the market-contract mode) and the system of coordinating such activity within a business firm (the internal-organization mode). The difference between these modes is best conveyed by an illustration, and the best illustration is perhaps that of rifle manufacture in Birmingham, England, in the 1860s as quoted by George Stigler (1968, 129).

> The master gun-maker--the entrepreneur--seldom possessed a factory or workshop.... Usually he owned merely a warehouse in the gun quarter, and his function was to acquire semi-finished parts and to give those out to specialized craftsmen, who undertook the assembly and finishing of the gun. He purchased material from the barrel-makers, lock-makers, sight-stampers, trigger-makers, ramrod-forgers, gun-furniture makers, and, if he were engaged in the military branch, from bayonet-forgers. All of these were independent manufacturers executing the orders of several master gun-makers.... Once the parts had been purchased from the "material-makers," as they were called, the next task was to hand them out to a long succession of "setters-up," each of whom performed a specific operation in connection with the assembly and finishing of the gun. To name only a few, there were those who prepared the front sight and lump end of the barrels; the jiggers, who attended to the breech end; the stockers, who let in the barrel and lock and shaped the stock; the barrel-strippers, who prepared the gun for rifling and proof; the hardeners, polishers, borers and riflers, engravers, browners, and finally the lock-freers, who adjusted the working parts (Allen 1929, 56-57).

This rather colorful description provides at least some sense of what it would mean to organize production entirely in the market-contract mode.[6] Each specialist owns his own tools (there is no separate capitalist who owns the means of production), and each's relationship with the master gun-maker is that of an independent contractor, not an employee. By contrast, production in the internal-organization mode would look much more like the factory system to which we are accustomed: tools and machinery would be owned not by the specialists themselves, but by a functionally distinct owner or owners (e.g., the stockholders), and the relationship of the specialist to the owner or owners would be not that of a contractor but of an employee.[7] Most real-world production is carried out in a way that mixes these two modes, but the ideal types are useful for theoretical purposes.

The issue facing the analyst of internal organization is: why do we observe one mode and not the other or, more generally, when should we expect to observe one mode and when the other? And the analysis proceeds in a manner parallel to--but in crucial respects different from--the analysis of incompatible uses of property rights.

The analyses are parallel in that they compare the transaction-cost properties of specific alternative institutional structures. They are different, however, in that the Coasean analysis of incompatible uses of property rights is largely a normative exercise while the analysis of internal organization is principally a descriptive matter. The former assesses the transaction-cost properties of the alternatives in order to investigate which is the cheaper or more efficient; the latter does the same but then goes on to use the conclusions about relative efficiency to explain why and predict when we should observe an organizational alternative. The dominant style of analysis in the literature of internal organization is implicitly (and sometimes explicitly) to presume that the reason we observe one mode of organization rather than the alternatives is that the observed mode is more efficient--in the sense of minimizing the sum of production costs and transaction costs--than those alternatives; the task then becomes one of scrutinizing the structure of transactions each alternative implies in order to determine the causes of this relative efficiency.[8] To explain, for example, why the internal-organization mode (in the sense described above) largely supplanted the market-contracting mode in production, one would typically ask what it is in the structure of transacting that makes the former less costly than the latter.

This is not necessarily an easy question. Indeed, by the standards of Coase (1960), the market-contract mode would seem to be an ideal system. Property rights are clearly defined; and transaction costs are low in the sense that face-to-face bargaining and exchange among the rights-holders is relatively easy. One early line of argument was to suggest that, while the market-contract mode was indeed entirely efficient in a more primitive state of technology, changes in the machinery of production ultimately made internal organization the more efficient alternative. This hoary explanation was placed within the Coasean framework by Alchian and Demsetz (1972), who argued that indivisibilities in the technology of production could lead to an externality problem akin to the "tragedy of the commons." Employing the externality shift in another guise, they showed that an externality arose in team production, not so much because the technology tied the workers together in some physical sense as because such technology made it difficult to determine each team member's marginal product and award him or her accordingly. As a result, efficiency would be enhanced under an alternate system in which one member of the team bought out the capital of his fellows, hired them to employment contracts, and, with the incentives of a residual claimant, undertook to monitor the team's output. In other words, the internal-organization mode is superior when technology creates the sorts of transaction costs associated with metering and monitoring team output.

This analysis is generally regarded as unexceptionable as far as it goes--which is not, unfortunately, very far. The problem is that we observe there to be far more internal organization than one could possibly explain on technological grounds. If the Alchian and Demsetz explanation were, in fact, the only explanation, we would not expect to see the internal-organization mode, but rather something nearer the market-contract mode in which individual specialists were replaced by small teams of specialists operating various indivisible parts of the production process. I think it is now generally agreed that "joint production can explain only a small fraction of the behavior of individuals associated with a firm" (Jensen and Meckling 1976, 310).[9]

As a result, theorists have had to look beyond indivisibilities for the source of the transaction costs that might explain the relative efficiency of the internal-organization modes we observe. A number of such sources have been proposed; but the alternative that seems lately to have won out is the notion of opportunism, often coupled with the suggestion that human information-processing abilities are limited (Williamson 1979; Klein, Crawford, and Alchian 1978; Monteverde and Teece 1982a, 1982b). Opportunism, as one might guess, is the ability of one party in a transaction to take self-seeking advantage of the other party, often as the result of superior information. Opportunistic behavior of this sort can lead to inefficiencies, and transactions subject to such opportunism might thus be carried out more efficiently if internalized within a single organization. The most important occasion for opportunism of this sort is when a transaction involves the commitment of resources in a highly specific or idiosyncratic way, leading to what Klein, Crawford, and Alchian (1978) call "appropriable quasirents."

Although it has never been fully articulated, it seems to me implicit in the literature that this question of specificity or idiosyncrasy is really of more fundamental theoretical interest than is opportunism--or even limited information-processing abilities--per se.[10] Indeed, I think the matter can be analyzed in terms of a clear theoretical distinction that, while not perhaps rendering the comparative-institutional approach to internal organization fully as elegant as general-equilibrium theory, at least provides that approach with a somewhat cleaner theoretical profile. At the same time, though, the distinction I will offer may also call for a reexamination of the efficiency approach to explaining modes of organization.

The Problem of Structural Knowledge

The reason that opportunism or similar effects may lead some modes of organization to be more efficient than others is that such opportunism somehow creates transaction costs of a particular kind. It is the nature of these transaction costs that we are concerned with in explaining the relative efficiency of institutional structures.

I suggested earlier that the notion of a transaction cost is often admitted to be somewhat fuzzy and hard to define. The most successful exegesis of the concept is probably that by Carl Dahlman, who teases out from Coase's discussion three categories of transaction cost: search and information costs, bargaining and decision costs, policing and enforcement costs. "Yet," says Dahlman, "this functional taxonomy of different transaction costs is unnecessarily elaborate: fundamentally, the three classes reduce to a single one--for they all have in common that they represent resource losses due to lack of information" (Dahlman 1979, 148). If one always knew the full extent of the transactions open to him, if one could always anticipate the terms offered and strategies used in bargaining, and if one always knew instantly whenever there occurred deviations from the agreed terms of contract, then transacting would always be costless.

I think this analysis of transaction costs is very much on target. But I also think that, having collapsed all such costs into the lack-of-information category, we now need to make new distinctions within this category if we are to explain internal-organization modes. What I propose is that there are two distinguishable types of lack of information. And only one of these provides an efficiency rationale for the existence of a significant degree of internal organization.

Perhaps the best way to see this is to begin by noticing that some sorts of lack of information are entirely consistent with a fully price-decentralized market-contract mode. In the extreme case of a general-equilibrium world, uncertainty of a specific kind is allowed for in the contingent-claims-contract formulation; yet, as Loasby (1976) and others have pointed out, there is no need whatever for internal modes of organization in such a world.

What sort of lack of information is implied here? The conception of ignorance and uncertainty in general-equilibrium theory--and indeed throughout the whole of neoclassical economics--is actually a very restricted and narrowly construed one. A definitive spokesman puts it this way. Uncertainty means "that we do not have a complete description of the world which we fully believe to be true. Instead, we consider the world to be in one or another of a range of states. Each state of the world is a description which is complete for all relevant purposes. Our uncertainty consists in not knowing which state is the true one" (Arrow 1974, 33). Uncertainty of this sort is incorporated into the maximization formalism in the following more-or-less-canonical fashion.[11] If $\underline{a}$ is the vector of possible actions an agent may engage in; $\{x_i\}$ is the set of states of the world the agent believes possible; $\{p_i\}$ is the set of (subjective) probabilities the agent associates with those possible states; and $U(\underline{a}|x_i)$ is a function relating the agent's utility to his actions and to the possible states of the world, then the agent's problem is

$$\max_{\underline{a}} \sum_i p_i U(\underline{a}|x_i),$$

i.e., to maximize the expected utility of his actions.

It is frequently instructive to compare the economist's definition of a term with the meaning that term holds in everyday discourse.[12] In this case, such an exercise begins to suggest why the economic definition is in fact so restricted a conception of uncertainty. Loasby puts it this way: "When someone says he is uncertain, what he usually means is not just that he doesn't know the chances of various outcomes, but that he doesn't know what outcomes are possible. He may well be far from sure even of the structure of the problem that he faces" (Loasby 1976, 9).[13]

What is often overlooked in the neoclassical literature of information and uncertainty is that its formalism implies certain-knowledge as much as it allows for uncertainty. The agent is implicitly presumed to have an exhaustive list of possible actions and states of the world and, equally important, a means/ends framework relating the actions and the states of the world to his utility. We might say that the agent has certain-knowledge of the structure of the problem he faces or, put another way, that he has perfect structural knowledge. Imperfections in the agent's knowledge extend only to specific parameters of the problem--the x_i--that are obscured from his vision.[14] He may have imperfect parametric knowledge but never imperfect structural knowledge; he may acquire parametric information but never structural information.

In some ways, the distinction I'm offering is not entirely novel; there have long been a number of similar-sounding distinctions floating around the literature, many of which come extremely near to what I'm driving at. But I also think that the words "structural" and "parametric" help avoid confusion and, more important, emphasize the essentially structural nature of knowledge.[15]

Perhaps the best known of these distinctions is Frank Knight's treatment of risk versus uncertainty (Knight 1971 [1921]).[16] It has been my experience that every economist believes he or she understands what Knight meant by this distinction--but that no two economists agree on what the distinction is. At one extreme are interpretations that see Knightian uncertainty as akin to structural uncertainty in my sense; at the other extreme are interpretations that see the issue as one of insurable versus uninsurable risk; and there are interpretations in between. My suspicion is that Knight intended something closer to the structural/parametric distinction; but in casting the matter in terms of one's ability to "calculate the probabilities," he opened the door to unnecessary confusion. So long as the categories are fully agreed upon, the noncalculability, subjectivity, or controversiality of probabilities per se provides no impediment to market contracting and therefore no rationale for internal organization; in fact, divergences of opinion about probabilities are an important source of gains from trade in contracting.[17]

The notion of imperfect structural knowledge is probably most akin to (and, of course, influenced by) the analysis of G.L.S. Shackle, who has long stressed the economic importance of the unknown, the unforeseen, and the unlistable (Shackle 1972). Shacklean uncertainty often goes by the name radical uncertainty. For the most part, however, Shackle's arguments have been taken (not entirely without justification) as attacks on our ability to theorize meaningfully about behavior under uncertainty. The semantics of structural uncertainty is intended to convey the opposite sense: to suggest--as I hope to articulate more fully below--that qualitative and categorical change is in fact susceptible to analysis within the proper theoretical framework. Moreover, the emphasis on structure is consistent with the view of knowledge taken in other fields and it may help counterbalance the excessively behavioristic interpretation of information to which economic modeling is often susceptible (Langlois 1983).18

Imperfect Structural Information and Internal Organization

None of what I've said so far need be interpreted as criticism of the mathematical optimization approach to information and uncertainty. The assumptions of that approach may well be entirely appropriate to its uses; I am not prepared here to argue that case one way or the other. My only contention is that if one restricts the notion of lack of information to mean merely an imperfection of what I have called parametric information, then one is never going to find the source of the transaction costs that provide internal modes of organization with a comparative-efficiency explanation.

Now, it is possible to use imperfections in parametric knowledge to generate an efficiency explanation for internal organization of a limited sort. Indeed, the Alchian and Demsetz argument is exactly of this form. The workers in a joint-production activity are united in a known-and-agreed-upon optimization problem: to maximize the value of their joint output. A critical parameter in this problem--the value of each team member's marginal product--is obscured from each agent's vision under a decentralized market-contract arrangement, and it is the residual claimant-monitor's superior knowledge of this parameter that makes the internal-organization form appear more efficient. But the problem, as we saw, is that this analysis cannot explain the full extent of internal organization.

Similarly, it is possible to construct models in which the internal-organization mode is more efficient than a decentralized market-contract mode because the former allows for better knowledge of a critical parameter like input availability (e.g., Arrow 1975). But such analyses are not typically comparative-institutional in form; rather, they take the market-failure approach, in which the nonoptimality of the market-contract mode is viewed as a presumption that the internal-organization mode is not merely more efficient but actually the only alternative. In fact, of course, there are normally a number of intermediate contracting modes and organizational alternatives available to handle these various imperfections in parametric information in a fashion at least as efficient as that of the pure internal-organization mode. For example, Williamson (1980) has argued that a decentralized contracting system using buffer inventories between successive stages of production is able to circumvent the inefficiencies attendant on uncertainties in input availability.

The point seems to me a quite general one. If the only imperfections in knowledge at stake were those of this parametric kind, then decentralized contracting would always be a cheap organizational alternative. This sort of imperfect information is precisely what state-contingent contracting, including the form practiced on organized futures markets, is all about. If all participants to a transaction really are aware of and certain about all the facts of the situation, and are in complete and detailed accord as to all possible contingencies, then decentralized market-contract arrangements should not be at a significant transaction-cost disadvantage.

Indeed, it is my suspicion that, in situations in which only parametric imperfections in information are involved, the market-contract mode--with the help of an organized futures market--is always at least as efficient as any other mode.[19] This is equivalent, in the terms of the comparative-efficiency logic of explanation, to a suspicion that imperfect parametric information of the sort treated in mathematical-optimization models can never provide an efficiency rationale for internal organization. I neither need nor wish to make an unequivocal stand on this point here.[20] Instead, I'd like to try to do the next best thing: to show that the leading efficiency explanation for internal organization--the danger of opportunism in contracting situations--can be reduced to and understood in terms of imperfection in structural knowledge.

The basic idea of the opportunism explanation is fairly simple: there can often arise contracting situations in which one or both parties to the contract is able to take advantage of informational asymmetries (including asymmetries he has himself created through some form of deception or dissembling) to effect a transfer of wealth from the other party to himself. A prime example of this is when one party has irreversibly committed resources to a production activity: the other party can then threaten to renege--and thereby inflict a capital loss on the first party--if that first party does not surrender some of the rents of his irreversible investment. When such opportunistic behavior is likely, the transaction will appear costly ex ante, and the alternative of organizing the activity internally becomes relatively more efficient.

The first thing to notice is that the source of the transaction costs here is not the self-interest-seeking aspect of opportunism: self-interest seeking is assumed present in, and indeed necessary for, even the most efficient instances of contracting. At the most fundamental level, the source of the transaction costs--once again--is a lack of information.

Williamson recognizes this point implicitly when he insists that opportunism is important only in conjunction with what, following Herbert Simon, he calls bounded rationality. "But for the simultaneous existence of both bounded rationality and opportunism," he writes, "all economic contracting problems are trivial and the study of economic institutions is unimportant" (Williamson 1981, 1545, emphasis in the original). What is "bounded rationality?" For present purposes it amounts to the notion that it is impossible to foresee all the relevant contingencies and therefore impossible to specify all such contingencies in a contract; therefore, contracts must often remain "incomplete."

Opportunism, in Williamson's analysis, is a distinct phenomenon that serves to make matters worse.

> Ubiquitous, albeit incomplete, contracting would nevertheless be feasible if economic agents were completely trustworthy. Principals would simply extract promises from agents that they will behave in a stewardship fashion, while agents would reciprocally ask principals to behave in good faith. Such devices will not work, however, if some economic actors (either principals or agents) are dishonest (or, more generally, disguise attributes or preferences, distort data, obfuscate issues, and otherwise confuse transactions) and it is very costly to distinguish opportunistic from nonopportunistic types ex ante (Williamson 1981, 1545).

The interpretation this passage suggests is that opportunism is indeed a parametric-information problem. One may be able to foresee all contingencies, but those contingencies include a state of the world labeled "opportunistic behavior"--and one doesn't know ahead of time whether or not that state will occur. This is the paradigmatic form of a parametric-information problem. And opportunism is thus a source of inefficiency in the same sense that a state of the world labeled "hurricane strikes agricultural region" would be a source of inefficiency: society would be wealthier if that state could not materialize (or, more generally, if it could be assigned a lower probability).21

All of this seems to me a valid and useful way to look at the problem of opportunism. But there remains an equally valid sense in which opportunism is not ultimately a problem of imperfect parametric information: for if there really were no imperfections in structural knowledge--if all contingencies really could be specified--then opportunism would be impossible.

In order to see why this is so, one first needs to get straight on what opportunism involves. If, as Williamson suggests, opportunism consists in taking advantage of one's ability generally to confuse, mislead, or dissemble, then, I would argue, this is already clearly a problem of imperfect structural knowledge: there is no meeting of the minds because the parties do not see the structure of their joint problem identically. Now, one may lie, dissemble, or obfuscate in regard merely to some parameter of an otherwise mutually agreed-upon problem--one's actual ability to produce a certain number of widgets, for example, or the true cost of some input. But surely this is the sort of informationally opportunistic behavior most easily (i.e., cheaply) dealt with in contract.

Consider in this connection the guise in which opportunism shows up most frequently: the holdup phenomenon associated with appropriable specialized quasirents (Klein, Crawford, and Alchian 1978; Goldberg 1976). Here the problem is that, once a contract is signed, one of the parties to it can exploit the specialized fixed investment of the other party by threatening to pull out of the contract; the opportunistic party may thus be able to appropriate some or all of the rents his transaction partner would otherwise lose if the deal did in fact dissolve. The question we must ask is: how is it that the two parties would have agreed _ex ante_ to a contract vulnerable in this way to opportunism _ex post_? And the answer has to be that the opportunism was unexpected in some sense. But in what sense? If we are to maintain the hypothesis that all contingencies are foreseen, it cannot be because the specific circumstances leading to the possibility of opportunism were not anticipated. That means that one party must have entered into the contracting knowing he might be exploited. Why would he do that? A possible answer--and one that I suspect is implicit in the literature--is that the vulnerable party had no choice, that is, accepting the contract even with the anticipated possibility of opportunism is the best alternative available to him.

Unhappily, this is not an entirely satisfactory story. First of all, to take it seriously--in a world in which all contingencies are foreseen--is to collapse the opportunism explanation into a monopoly explanation. If my entering into a contract will result in a specialized investment, and if _ex ante_ there are few potential contracting partners, then I may be forced to accept the danger of opportunistic expropriation or invest resources to prevent expropriation (e.g., by using a more flexible but more expensive technique of production); as a result, internal organization may be a more efficient way to organize the transaction. But the costliness of contracting arises not because of opportunism but because of the ex ante fewness of transaction alternatives. As Demsetz pointed out in a related context, the specialized nature of an investment ex post leads to inefficiency only if there is inadequate competition ex ante[22] (Demsetz 1968). The monopoly explanation of internal organization certainly provides an efficiency rationale for internal organization; but it is at best a partial explanation, since we observe much--if not most--internal organization in situations that are competitive in this ex ante sense.

Now, one might argue that, ex ante competition notwithstanding, the creation of a specialized asset results in problems of opportunism (a) at the time of contract renewal or (b) to the extent that one can renege on a contract with legal impunity.[23] But such an argument would make my point even clearer. Barring an outright failure of the legal system to enforce explicit contracts (or a persistent and systematic inappropriateness in that system's awards of damage for breach of contract), the only way one can renege on a contract with impunity is if the specifications it contains are vague or incomplete--that is to say, only if the informational problem involved is one of imperfect structural knowledge.[24] Opportunism at contract renewal is certainly a real problem. But why is it necessary to renew the contract? If all contingencies were foreseeable in complete detail, one could easily write a long-term contract--indeed, an infinitely long-term contract in the limit--and the problems of opportunism at contract renewal would be entirely eliminated at no cost. The reason that long-term contracts are infeasible or expensive, of course, is that one cannot foresee all contingencies in detail in advance. Which is precisely my point. The reigning comparative-efficiency explanation for internal organization ultimately reduces to an explanation from imperfect structural knowledge.

Organization and Efficiency: A Reinterpretation

If by now the reader is, as I hope, persuaded that the distinction between structural and parametric knowledge is a valid one, and that it is the former to which we should look in explaining the transaction-cost underpinnings of internal organization, he or she may nonetheless wonder why the distinction is an important one. Why is it significant that the most solid--and perhaps even the only--comparative-efficiency explanations for internal organization ultimately trace to the notion of structural knowledge?

The answer, I would suggest, is that to see changes in structural knowledge as important to economic explanation is necessarily to alter the nature of such explanation.

I have been careful throughout this essay to highlight the logic of explanation that (implicitly or explicitly) lies behind the modern comparative-institutional approach to the theory of internal organization. That logic, once again, is of a comparative-efficiency sort: one postulates two or more discrete institutional alternatives and assesses their relative efficiency by considering the transaction-cost properties of each. To isolate the transaction costs that make an observed organizational form the most efficient of those considered is, according to this implicit logic, to have explained not only the economic nature of that form but also why it is observed. What I would now like to suggest is that this logic of explanation necessarily becomes inappropriate if the possibility of changing structural knowledge is admitted into the analysis.

The methodological issues involved are rather complex, and I've attempted to deal with them more carefully elsewhere (Langlois 1982a). But it may be sufficient for present purposes simply to consider what it means for something to be efficient. In its most general sense, a structure (an organizational form, let us say) is efficient if it achieves a goal or end at the least cost possible--at the least sacrifice of valued resources. One organizational structure is more efficient than another if it achieves the same goal at a lower cost. In order to explain the nature of a structure in efficiency terms, then, one has, at a minimum, to be able to specify the goal with respect to which the structure is to be evaluated and the means on which it economizes in attempting to achieve the goal; to put it more simply, one has to specify a means/ends framework, a problem to which the structure is a solution. In order to explain the existence of a structure--efficient or otherwise--one has to do even more: one has to specify a mechanism by which one believes the structure to have been brought about and maintained (Ullmann-Margalit 1978).

Standard neoclassical theory, especially in its more formal manifestations, provides us with a logic of explanation in which these two specifications are made simultaneously. The structure in question here is the whole of the price system; and the efficiency of that system is judged by its ability to allocate a specified set of resources in Pareto-optimal fashion according to a given set of preference orderings. The mechanism that (under appropriate circumstances) brings this efficient result about is the efficient behavior of all the economic agents in the system, who consciously seek to allocate their individual resources within the known and given commodity space so as to maximize their individual levels of utility. Admittedly, this is an odd sort of explanatory mechanism: rather than literally proposing a process by which the efficient result is achieved, it relies simply on showing that the efficient result is logically possible given the assumptions. My purpose, however, is not to criticize this logic of explanation on its own grounds but merely to show that it is inapplicable under the assumption of changing structural knowledge.

In its most rigorous form, this neoclassical mode of explanation is entirely an axiomatic exercise. That is to say, conclusions about the efficiency properties of the system as a whole are deduced from axioms about the behavior of the individuals within the system. This approach is what F. A. Hayek long ago described as the "pure logic of choice" (Hayek 1972 [1948]). As he quite correctly pointed out, conclusions can be said to follow logically only from propositions that are simultaneously present in the same mind. Therefore, to draw conclusions about the efficiency properties of the system as a whole from axioms about the behavior of individuals is implicitly to see a system operating as if all relevant knowledge were given to a single central mind. An equivalent way to put this point, I believe, is that the axiomatic approach necessarily implies or requires that all economic agents have complete and perfect structural knowledge.

An axiomatic neoclassical model can make statements about the efficiency of a structure because (a) it postulates a fixed and specified global allocation problem in terms of which efficiency may be judged and (b) it provides a picture of how--through the conscious efforts of agents to solve their own individual efficiency problems--this global allocation problem is solved. Imperfect parametric knowledge creates no particular difficulties for this approach: both the global and the local optimizations are fully meaningful in a state-contingent probabilistic formulation. But imperfect or incomplete structural knowledge is quite another matter. If, on level (a), the analyst is aware of only part of the structural features of the global allocation problem against which he would judge efficiency, then his conclusions are necessarily suspect: the structure under study may be efficient relative to what is known, but grossly inefficient relative to what is unknown. Similarly, if, on level (b), the problem-structures of the individual agents do not overlap more-or-less completely with the global problem-structure, then one cannot logically (axiomatically) connect the individual problems with the global one. This is essentially Hayek's point.

In a sense, the problem I'm pointing to has not gone entirely unnoticed. It is actually the much-discussed absence-of-complete-futures-markets problem in another guise. Students of general-equilibrium theory have long recognized that the efficiency properties of the systems they construct depend on the existence of complete markets for all commodities under all possible future states of the world. This circumstance appears particularly troubling when one notices that there are clearly markets whose existence is logically impossible: how could there be markets, speculative or otherwise, for commodities as yet undreamed of?

Most writings on welfare economics deal with the absence-of-complete-markets problem by simply ignoring it. When the problem does crop up in the writings of general-equilibrium theorists, it is most often portrayed as a message that the economic system has been shown to be inefficient. But this is a very misleading interpretation. A more accurate characterization would be that the incompleteness of structural knowledge makes it impossible to assess the market in efficiency terms. To suggest that the economic system is an evolving or learning process in which new knowledge is constantly being created is to suggest that there does not exist a fixed allocational problem against which efficiency may be judged. Efficiency, at least insofar as it implies a comparison with some postulated global allocation problem, is simply the wrong standard. The economy is not inefficient because of imperfect structural knowledge; it is simply a-efficient. The reality is not wrong because it doesn't fit the model; the model is inapplicable because it doesn't fit the reality.

Now, one may wish to argue that, for basic price-and-allocation theory in some of its forms, the difficulties of incomplete structural knowledge may be safely ignored, allowing one to go on talking meaningfully about efficiency in the usual way. But one cannot argue this with respect to the theory of internal organization--at least if one accepts my assertion that changing structural knowledge is at the heart of that theory.

What, then, is to be done? The answer, it seems to me, lies in recognizing that the neoclassical logic of explanation is not the only one available. Indeed, to talk about changes in structural knowledge is virtually to imply the alternative I have already suggested: an evolutionary logic of explanation. For to speak of evolution in a cultural (as distinct from a biological) setting is necessarily to be concerned with learning and the production of new knowledge (Hayek 1967, 1973, 1978; Boulding 1978, 1981; Nelson and Winter 1982). And evolution in any context is about the nature of change in organized structures.

What would be the effect of moving to this alternate explanatory framework? For example, would it require giving up the notion of efficiency entirely? The answer is: not necessarily. Efficiency has a place in an evolutionary theory, even if it is a more limited place than some economists seem to think; and it does seem to me possible to reinterpret the efficiency concept sensibly in an evolutionary context. At the same time, however, this reinterpretation immediately raises some theoretical issues that may have substantive implications for the way we analyze alternative institutional structures.

Evolutionary thought applied to economic matters is a pastime surely as old as economics itself; indeed, if Hayek (1973, 23) is right, biologists got the idea from social scientists rather than the other way around. There have certainly been inappropriate and mistaken applications of evolutionary thought to social science, as much perhaps now as in the past (Hayek 1978). But there has also lately arisen a good deal of interest in a coherent and more sophisticated version of the evolutionary approach,[25] one that largely avoids the errors and excesses to which this line of reasoning is often heir. It is not my intention to justify this literature here, or even to describe the theory in much detail. But a brief outline of the basic ideas should illustrate how this approach differs from the axiomatic optimization/allocation logic of explanation.

In a paradigmatic general-equilibrium model, what holds the world together is the conscious means/ends rationality of the economic agents. Not so in the evolutionary paradigm. Here the growth and maintenance of economic organization is explained in terms of three factors: mutation (or variation); selection; and memory. It is the last two of these operating in conjunction that could be said to hold the world together in this model. Selection is the system-wide factor, analogous to (but, of course, ultimately quite different from) the postulated global allocation problem that connects things together in the neoclassical model. Memory is a property of the economic agents in the model, even if a somewhat passive factor normally seen in terms of habit, routine,[26] or the following of rules--rules that may often be unconscious or tacit in the manner of Michael Polanyi (1958).

None of this requires rationality of the means/ends sort; as a consequence, none of this requires the assumption of preexisting utility functions, of a fixed and given menu of alternatives, or, most to the point, of perfect structural knowledge on the part of the agents. What it does mean is that stable economic organization is possible even in the absence of such perfect structural knowledge.[27]

Moreover, the mutation (or variation) function provides a mechanism by which new structural knowledge is brought into the system. The mutation factor is also the province of the economic agent,[28] and it is a function that, in contrast to the memory function, portrays the agent not only more active than does the neoclassical alternative but also as quite fully as rational as the more conventional economic man--even if saying this requires that we rethink our definition of what it means to be rational.[29]

How does efficiency enter into this logic of explanation? In a way that is at once subtle and crucial. There is a long-standing debate in biology about the logical status of Darwinian theory. Some writers have claimed that the theory of biological evolution is tautological--that survival is its own explanation. According to this argument, the fitness of an organism to its environment is defined by the ability of the organism to survive; and fitness is then used to explain why the organism in fact survived. Modern Darwinians respond to this charge by suggesting that survival is not in fact the appropriate definition of fitness; one can and should invoke an independent criterion--an efficiency criterion--to explain why an organism is able to survive in a particular environment. To these biologists, "certain morphological, physiological, and behavioral traits should be superior a priori as designs for living in new environments. These traits confer fitness by an engineer's criterion of good design, not by the empirical fact of their survival and spread. It got colder before the woolly mammoth evolved its shaggy coat" (Gould 1977, 42). This, then, is the role of efficiency in the explanation of alternative organizational forms: a transaction cost analysis provides the "engineer's criterion of good design" that suggests why a structure is well (or at least adequately) adapted to its environment. In other words, we need to reinterpret the meaning of a comparative-efficiency analysis in terms of what, in other disciplines, would be described as a kind of functional analysis. That this is in one sense an a priori standard of fitness does not by any means imply, however, that the evolutionary logic of explanation and the axiomatic efficiency approach are therefore equivalent or interchangeable. Herbert Simon has put the matter nicely.

> In practice, it is very rarely that the existence or character of institutions are <u>deduced</u> from the functions that must be performed for system survival. In almost all cases it is the other way round; it is empirical observation of the behavior pattern that raises the question of why it persists--what function it performs. Perhaps, in an appropriate axiomatic formulation, it would be possible to <u>deduce</u> that every society must have food-gathering institutions. In point of fact, such institutions can be <u>observed</u> in every society, and their existence is then rationalized by the argument that obtaining food is a functional requisite for all societies. This kind of argument may demonstrate the sufficiency of a particular pattern for performing the essential function, but cannot demonstrate its necessity--cannot show that there may not be alternative, functionally equivalent, behavior patterns that would satisfy the same need (Simon 1978, 4; emphasis in the original).

An efficiency analysis of organizational forms is thus a kind of <u>ex post</u> reconstruction. It is an attempt to demonstrate the rationale for what exists by superimposing after the fact an axiomatic framework on a structure that could not have been predicted <u>ex ante</u> from such a framework. This reflects the cleavage between explanation and prediction that is characteristic of evolutionary theory (Scriven 1959).

What does it mean to talk about the relative efficiency of alternative organizational modes? Once we have reconstructed a means/ends framework to interpret in axiomatic terms the function served by an organizational form, we can then use the same framework to compare the efficiency of the alternatives. This should be a meaningful exercise so long as we use the same framework consistently--and so long as the framework we have chosen adequately captures the environment in question. (More on this point shortly.)

This does not mean, however, that we can ever portray an organizational mode as optimal, except perhaps in a very narrow sense of the term. Since structural knowledge is admitted to be incomplete in an evolutionary story, there must always remain alternatives yet to be invented that may perform the function in question more efficiently than do the known alternatives.[30] A functionalist interpretation of efficiency claims can never justify the contention that we live in the best of all possible worlds.[31]

Two Implications

It is important to notice that this functionalist reinterpretation is an explanation only in one of two possible senses. As I've already suggested, a logic of explanation operates at two levels. On one level it is concerned with the nature or function of a structure--with the design characteristics that sustain it in its environment. On another level, a logic of explanation is or can be concerned with the origin of the structure--with the mechanism by which it came into existence (Ullmann-Margalit 1978). On the first level, as we've seen, the comparative-efficiency approach, reinterpreted in functionalist terms, is relatively unproblematical. It is on the second level that problems begin to set in.

Here I would identify two substantive difficulties: (a) the disequilibrium problem and (b) the path-dependency problem.

The first problem--which also operates on the functional level--is this: efficiency is necessarily defined relative to the environment in which the firm is operating. As a result, it is crucial that one specify the environment correctly in assessing the relative efficiency of alternate modes. If we take equilibrium to mean a state in which structural knowledge remains (perhaps temporarily) constant and disequilibrium to mean a situation in which relevant structural knowledge is changing, then the meaning of efficiency--and the nature of what is efficient--will depend upon whether we see the environment in question as an equilibrium or disequilibrium one. The mode of organization that minimizes the sum of production and transaction costs in equilibrium need not be the one that does so out of equilibrium. To the extent, then, that an organized structure faces a range of environments, the efficient mode will vary with time. Indeed, we need to be especially careful in judging organizational efficiency in terms of the environment we observe at any moment of time--for if that environment is likely to change, an organizational mode adapted to the environment of the moment may well be maladapted in some larger sense. This is the essence of the idea that there is a trade-off between flexibility and efficiency (Loasby 1976; B.H. Klein 1977): that flexibility is in fact efficient in a changing environment, since an inflexible (albeit otherwise efficient) structure has a transaction-cost disadvantage in such an environment.

With this in mind, it may be useful to return to the arguments about structural knowledge that I offered earlier. If my interpretation is correct, then what students of internal organization are pointing to is that internal organization modes are more efficient than market-contract modes in situations where structural knowledge is incomplete--and therefore where the environment is changing. Conversely, market-contract modes may actually be more efficient in situations where the incompleteness of structural knowledge is less important--and thus where the environment is relatively stable. This is a substantive implication that could presumably be subjected to careful empirical and historical analysis.

But there is more to the story. And it is here that the second level--the "originary" level--of explanation becomes important. For it is one thing to assert at a functional level that a mode of organization is most efficient under specified circumstances and quite another thing to have explained why we observe a particular mode actually to exist. Which mode we observe will depend not only on its a priori superiority over other known modes but also on the specific historical sequence that the evolutionary process followed. For "the existence of such structures may in fact depend not only on [the] environment, but also on the existence in the past of many other environments, indeed on a definite sequence of such environments. . . . " (Hayek 1967, 75). A mode must not only be efficient now; it must also have been efficient throughout its history.

Conceivably, then, we might compare two institutional alternatives (like internal and market-contract forms of organization) and find neither with a claim to be more adapted to the environment in question; we might even find that the arrangement we do not observe is in fact superior on some grounds to the one we observe and wish to explain.

Consider this scenario. Suppose, on grounds already suggested, that the internal organization mode is not superior to a market-contract mode in a stable environment in which states of knowledge are not changing and in which the categories of action are known to and agreed upon by all participants. Why then might we still observe internal organization modes rather than market-contract arrangements? One answer might be that, although internal organization is no more efficient--and maybe even less efficient--in the current stable environment, economic history passed through periods in which structural knowledge did change rapidly; and internal organization modes were able to maintain a persistent structure during the passage, whereas the market-contract alternative did not survive these periods.[32] And if there is no mechanism we can point to by which the failed modes are reestablished once equilibrium is restored, then the internal modes will continue to be observed even if less efficient in a functional sense.[33]

This is not an entirely implausible scenario. We can think of independent (good design) reasons why one or another internal organization mode would be better able to adapt to changing circumstances. A mode of organization can be thought of as a kind of memory system. In the gun-making example cited earlier, the decentralized market-contract mode "remembers" how to make guns. Like a firm, it evolved what organization theorists sometimes describe as an operational program--a way of doing things, a corpus of rules for action. But, unlike a firm, this pure market system lacks some of the higher-level functions of memory. To put it slightly differently, it lacks not so much the ability to learn as the ability to remain an identified whole while learning--to co-evolve. Frank Knight, who is remembered for having had a differential risk-aversion explanation for firms, actually saw the matter in a way very close to what I've just suggested.[34]

> When uncertainty is present and the task of deciding what to do and how to do it takes the ascendancy over that of execution, the internal organization of the productive group is no longer a matter of indifference or a mechanical detail. Centralization of this deciding and controlling function is imperative, a process of "cephalization," such as has taken place in the evolution of organic life, is inevitable, and for the same reasons as in the case of biological evolution (Knight 1971, 268).

This zones-of-disequilibrium explanation is another substantive implication of looking at internal organization in a dynamic context, and it also calls for empirical and historical examination.[35]

NOTES

1 For example: Alchian and Demsetz (1972); Fama (1980); Jensen and Meckling (1976); Klein, Crawford, and Alchian (1978); Teece (1980, 1982a, 1982b); and Williamson (1975, 1979, 1980, 1981).

2 For an elaboration of this distinction between the welfare-economic and the Coasean approaches, see, for example, Demsetz (1969) and Dahlman (1979).

3 The canonical locus of this view is Nelson and Winter (1982); but see also O'Driscoll and Rizzo (1984). For a survey, see Langlois (1982a).

4 An exception was Frank Knight (1971 [1921]).

5 In fact, a close reading of "The Nature of the Firm" shows that Coase's explanation for firms ultimately reduces to what I describe here as incomplete structural knowledge. I have gone through the exegetics of this argument in an earlier working paper (Langlois 1981).

6 Even this is not the purest example we could imagine. In this story, the entrepreneur presumably owns the gun parts throughout the process and merely rents the labor of each specialist (who owns his own tools), paying him on a per-piece basis. But we could imagine a world in which each specialist sold the partly finished product outright to the specialists in the next stage of production, who in turn sold the more nearly finished product to the specialists in the next stage, etc. Many other variants are possible, of course. For a catalogue, see Williamson (1980).

7 The distinction between an employee contract or employee relationship and a contractor relationship lies in the specificity of the agreement between the parties. A contractor is paid to provide a relatively specific service, and his remuneration is tied to performance of the service (e.g., a piece rate for gun parts). An employee is paid to perform any of a range of services at the employer's discretion. More formally, the employee performs any service $x \in X$, where X is a set of possible services mutually agreed to by employer and employee and x, which may vary over time, is the specific service chosen by the employer. One could think of X as a detailed position description. Those who conceive of X as explicitly known and bargained over talk of the employment contract; those who recognize the extent of X to be more tacitly understood or implicit in nature talk of the employment relation, a term that, in any case, is preferable to the more loaded "authority relation" (Cf. Williamson 1975, 71-72).

8 It is in this way that the modern theory of internal organization attempts to elude the charge of tautology often leveled at Coase's 1937 analysis (e.g., by Alchian and Demsetz 1972). By finding an indepen-

dent explanation of efficiency in terms of the transactional structure, one avoids the appearance of first defining relative efficiency as the ability to supplant an alternative mode of organization and then using the concept of efficiency to explain why one mode supplanted another. This issue will surface again below in a slightly different guise.

9 Williamson (especially 1975, ch. 5) has shown in general that technological interdependencies among stages of production is neither a necessary nor a sufficient condition for internal organization. Much that is technologically separable is not efficiently handled by market contracts, and some processes that are technologically linked can in fact be coordinated efficiently through contracting. Teece (1980) has made a similar argument for economies of scope, suggesting that the presence of economies of scope in the production function has few implications by itself for the scope of internal organization.

10 This is especially clear in the work of Teece (1982a, 1982b), who stresses the importance of idiosyncratic--and often tacit--knowledge in the analysis of specialized assets.

11 For an excellent survey of the mathematical economics of information and uncertainty, see Hirshleifer and Riley (1979).

12 The term "competition" is, of course, another--and closely related--example.

13 The view of uncertainty Loasby here describes has long been urged on the profession by G.L.S. Shackle (on whom see below). This broader view of uncertainty also tends to crop up in the work of writers interested in innovation and technological change. In addition to Loasby, see, for example, B.H. Klein (1977) and Schon (1971).

14 Of course, one may represent the agent as uncertain as between a number of given problem structures (Cf. Marschak and Radner 1972, 12-13); but this just pushes the structural knowledge problem one level higher.

15 Indeed, my principal motivation for offering this structural/parametric distinction is to provide a new language for--a new way of talking about--aspects of economic behavior that might be treated in other ways (e.g., under the rubric of "bounded rationality"). For example, many of the implications I will draw from this distinction might also be drawn from a formulation in which there is perfect structural knowledge--but in which that known structure is so complex that the agent acts in effect as if he were uncertain of the structure. This is essentially Herbert Simon's well-known formulation. In emphasizing complexity and information-processing abilities alone, however, one has not strayed very far from the neoclassical maximization paradigm; in fact, "bounded rationality" in Simon's sense can be reduced to neoclassical optimization (Baumal and Quandt 1964). By contrast, the structural/parametric terminology helps to underscore the extra-neoclassical side of the phenomenon and thus helps to make clearer the pattern of argument. This I am attempting to draw in this paper.

16 A similar distinction was drawn between case probability (uncertainty) and class probability (risk) by Ludwig von Mises (1949). (For a discussion of the probabilistic analyses of Knight, Mises, and G.L.S.

Shackle in light of modern subjective probability theory, see Langlois (1982b).) More recently, Teece (1982a) has drawn attention to Koopmans' distinction between primary uncertainty and secondary uncertainty (Koopmans 1957, 162-163). While this distinction is no doubt an important one, it does not seem to be a distinction between types of uncertainty but between sources of uncertainty. Primary uncertainty appears to mean uncertainty that arises from exogenous sources like discoveries about nature or changes in preferences; secondary uncertainty seems to mean uncertainty generated within the economic system itself by one agent's imperfect information about the decisions being taken simultaneously by other agents.

17 This assertion anticipates in part the argument of the next section.

18 We are fortunate that the late Fritz Machlup has left behind a mostly completed manuscript on the semantics of information and knowledge in the sciences (Machlup 1983). A close reading of this manuscript suggests that the structural/parametric distinction nowhere runs afoul of Machlup's gentle strictures on usage and is in fact quite consistent with ideas elsewhere in the information sciences broadly construed. As Machlup points out, the idea of form is closely related to the idea of information, since the word's Latin root means "to put into form." And he quotes approvingly this passage from Boulding: ". . . we cannot regard knowledge as simply the accumulation of information in a stockpile, even though all messages that are received by the brain may leave some sort of deposit there. Knowledge must itself be regarded as a structure, a very complex and frequently quite loose pattern, . . . with its parts connected in various ways by ties of varying degrees of strength. Messages are continually shot into this structure; some of them pass right through its interstices (. . .) without effecting any perceptible change in it. Sometimes messages 'stick' to the structure and become part of it. . . . Occasionally, however, a message which is inconsistent with the basic pattern of the mental structure, but which is of a nature that it cannot be disbelieved hits the structure, which is then forced to undergo a complete reorganization" (Boulding 1955, 103-104).

19 I am excluding Alchian-and-Demsetz situations in which, for purely technological reasons, individual property rights cannot be clearly defined.

20 The reason for my diffidence is that I can think of no better way to prove the assertion than by example and counterexample. If you give me a case of imperfect parametric information in which internal organization appears clearly more efficient than the market-contract mode, I can show either (a) that the situation really involves a problem of structural knowledge or (b) there exists an intermediate contractual alternative that is just as efficient. But this is not the best sort of proof one could wish for.

21 This is one way to understand some of the now-popular arguments about how cultural factors give Japan certain economic advantages. Because Japanese culture places a premium on non-opportunistic behavior in economic relations, the argument goes, fewer resources are wasted in guarding against opportunism, and contracting is less costly in that country. In fact, one apparently does see greater use of subcontract-

ing in Japanese industry than in American (but one also sees a good deal of internal organization). Schotter (1981) uses a recurrent-game model to analyze the ability of social norms and cultural conventions to reduce transaction costs. The brand-name capital effect popularized by Benjamin Klein (1974) is a closely related idea.

22 In fact, I would argue, the correctness of Demsetz's argument depends on the assumption of perfect structural knowledge--but this is, of course, the assumption I am now operating under.

23 By this I mean that one can break a contract without being forced to pay damages equal to the capital loss the breach inflicts on the owner of the specialized asset. For an argument that this is the correct economic measure of damages in breach of contract, see, e.g., Posner (1977, 88-93).

24 This is, in fact, the form in which imperfect structural knowledge most often enters the theory of internal organization--and law and economics more generally. One knows the general form of the relevant categories, but one is qualitatively ignorant of the specific subcategories. For example, I might contract with you to build a jet airpane; but, while we both know (at least tacitly) what a jet airplane is, we are unable to specify <u>ex ante</u> all the attributes of the plane. As Teece (1982a) points out, it is impossible by definition to specify in a contract a complex product that does not yet exist. O'Driscoll and Rizzo (1984) discuss this problem in terms of the distinction between the typical and the unique features of an event. "We anticipate events as to their typicality," they write, "but cannot fill in the 'details' beforehand. Neoclassical economics . . . has evaded the distinction between uniqueness and typicality. Those aspects of events are conflated when each possible situation or outcome is 'condensed' into a single scalar quantity. From this perspective we delude ourselves into thinking that we have fully characterized the event and thus eliminated the open-endedness of the future. In reality, we have characterized only a single typical feature of the event in question and ignored everything else."

25 I am thinking especially of the ideas of Hayek (1967, 1973, 1978) and Boulding (1978, 1981) on the philosophical level and the efforts of Nelson and Winter (1982) to transform evolutionary ideas into a viable affirmative research program.

26 Memory, as Sidney Winter alliteratively would have it, consists in "routines as genes" (Winter 1964, 1975).

27 Indeed, as Heiner (1983) has argued from a quite different angle, stable patterns of behavior are not only consistent with generalized uncertainty but actually the product of such uncertainty. Heiner's highly original formulation is consistent with much of my argument, but a more detailed discussion is beyond the scope of this paper.

28 Mutation in economics often goes under the name of "entrepreneurship." For theories of entrepreneurship compatible with this logic of explanation, see Schumpeter (1934, 1942) and Kirzner (1973).

29 The means/ends conception of rationality in neoclassical theory is grounded in the rationalist tradition that sees reason solely as in-

volving conscious logical reasoning from known premises. In contrast to this view is an equally hoary tradition in which "reason had meant the capacity to recognize truth . . . when [one meets] it, rather than a capacity of deductive reasoning from explicit premises" (Hayek 1967, 84). These two traditions are related to, if not exactly identical with, Herbert Simon's distinction between substantive and procedural rationality (Simon 1978). For a discussion, see Langlois (1982a).

30 Of course, one way to reconcile a world of imperfect parametric knowledge with a global-efficiency conception of economics is simply to define as a transaction cost any lack of knowledge or information that prevents the exploitation of a profit opportunity. Thus, for example, one could argue that any given organizational form (or anything else, for that matter) is necessarily optimal when all transaction costs are considered--for the fact that undiscovered superior alternatives are not in use is simply a reflection of the transaction costs of discovering those unknown alternatives. Needless to say, this closed version of the transaction-cost paradigm, which appears in the literature from time to time, is merely tautological. I am implicitly adhering to the open version of the paradigm in which, for reasons already suggested, transaction costs are independently defined and in which not everything impeding hypothetical optimality is ipso facto a transaction cost.

31 In saying this, let me also note that the evolutionary approach to analyzing organizational modes is no less antagonistic to certain forms of rationalist radicalism than to rationalist justifications of the status quo. The reason is that, while we don't live in the best of all possible worlds, what exists is not therefore arbitrary. An evolutionary view recognizes the empirical character of economic knowledge and sees strong constraints on our ability consciously to remake complex social organizations at will (Cf. Hayek 1973).

32 This point (that disequilibrium may result in the selecting out of those who would otherwise have been most efficient in the ultimate equilibrium) has been made in a slightly different context by Winter (1964).

33 The mechanism by which failed alternative modes might reestablish themselves would, of course, be entrepreneurship--economic mutation. As Alchian pointed out long ago, local search may not be an adequate mechanism to the extent--as seems likely in dealing with discrete institutional alternatives--that there are "non-convexities" involved in moving from one alternative to another (Alchian 1950); but this does not preclude a demonstration that search (or entrepreneurship more generally) of a nonlocal kind is at work. If one could show that it is not costly to try out failed alternatives from the past and that people are, in fact, continually trying out these alternatives, then the fact that a particular mode continues its dominance offers a far greater presumption that it is the most efficient of those known. But notice that this is an imminent argument, not a functionalist argument. Confusing the two levels of discourse--the functionalist explanation and the originary explanation--is a pastime pervasive in economics; this tendancy can perhaps be traced to Milton Friedman's well-known instrumentalist defense of marginalism, which can be understood as an attempt to install as a methodological dictum precisely this confusion between levels of explanation.

34 I think cephalization rather than centralization is really the operative notion here. The issue Knight is getting at is flexibility--not central authority or planning in the manner of, say, Galbraith. For, as Hayek notes, neither the ability to learn nor the appearance of purposiveness depends quite as strongly on centralized direction as one might think. "There is," he writes, "no reason why a polycentric order in which each element is guided only by rules and receives no orders from a centre should not be capable of bringing about as complex and apparently as 'purposive' an adaptation to circumstances as could be produced in a system where a part is set aside to preform such an order on an analogue or model before it is put into execution by the larger structure. Insofar as the self-organizing forces of a structure as a whole lead at once to the right kind of action (or to tentative actions which can be retracted before too much harm is done) such a single-stage order need not be inferior to a hierarchic one in which the whole merely carries out what has first been tried out in a part. Such a non-hierarchic order dispenses with the necessity of first communicating all the information on which its several elements act to a common centre and conceivably may make the use of more information possible than could be transmitted to, and digested by, a centre" (Hayek 1967, 74).

35 In fact, there is reason to think that the gun-making case cited above may itself provide a good example. As Stigler remarks, "[t]he later history of the gun trade, in which American innovations in production techniques were revolutionary, suggest[s] that the organization in Birmingham was deficient in its provision for technical experimentation (Stigler 1968, 1951, 140n). I should also note that some authors have, in fact, focused on innovation in explaining internal organization; see especially Teece (1982a).

REFERENCES

1 Alchian, A., Uncertainty, evolution, and economic theory, Journal of Political Economy 58:3 (1950) 211-221.

2 Alchian, A. and Demsetz, H., Production, information costs, and economic organization, American Economic Review 62:5 (December, 1972).

3 Allen, G.C., The Industrial Development of Birmingham and the Black Country, 1906-1927 (London, 1929) 56-57.

4 Arrow, K., The Limits of Organization (Norton, New York, 1974).

5 Arrow, K., Vertical integration and communication, Bell Journal of Economics 6:1 (Spring, 1975).

6 Baumol, W.J. and Quandt, R.E., Rules of thumb and optimally imperfect decisions, American Economic Review 54 (1964) 23-46.

7 Boulding, K.E., Notes on the information concept, Explorations (Toronto) 6 (1955) 103-112.

8 Boulding, K.E., Ecodynamics: A New Theory of Societal Evolution (Sage Publications, Beverly Hills, 1978).

9 Boulding, K.E., Evolutionary Economics (Sage Publications, Beverly Hills, 1981).

10 Coase, R.H., The nature of the firm, Economica, N.S. 4 (November 1937).

11 Coase, R.H., The problem of social cost, Journal of Law and Economics 3 (October, 1960).

12 Dahlman, C., The problem of externality, Journal of Law and Economics 22 (1979) 141-162.

13 Demsetz, H., Why regulate utilities?, Journal of Law and Economics 11 (1968) 55-66.

14 Demsetz, H., Information and efficiency: another viewpoint, Journal of Law and Economics 12 (1969) 1.

15 Fama, E.F., Agency problems and the theory of the firm, Journal of Political Economy 88:2 (1980) 288-307.

16 Goldberg, V., Regulation and administered contracts, Bell Journal of Economics 7:2 (1976) 426-452.

17 Gould, S.J., Ever Since Darwin (Norton, New York, 1977).

18 Hayek, F.A., Individualism and Economic Order (University of Chicago Press, Chicago, 1948; Gateway edition, 1972).

19 Hayek, F.A., Studies in Philosophy, Politics, and Economics (University of Chicago Press, Chicago, 1967).

20 Hayek, F.A., Law, Legislation, and Liberty, Vol. 1: Rules and Order (University of Chicago Press, Chicago, 1973).

21 Hayek, F.A., The Three Sources of Human Values, Epilogue to Law, Legislation, and Liberty, Vol. 3 (University of Chicago Press, Chicago, 1978).

22 Heiner, R.A., The origin of predictable behavior, American Economic Review 73:4 (1983) 560-595.

23 Hirshleifer, J. and Riley, J.G., The analytics of uncertainty and information--an expository survey, Journal of Economic Literature 17 (1979).

24 Jensen, M.C. and Meckling, W.H., Theory of the firm: managerial behavior, agency costs and ownership structure, Journal of Financial Economics 3 (1976) 305-360.

25 Kirzner, I.M., Competition and Entrepreneurship (University of Chicago Press, Chicago, 1973).

26 Klein, B., The competitive supply of money, Journal of Money, Credit, and Banking 6 (1974) 423.

27 Klein, B., Crawford, R.G. and Alchian, A., Vertical integration, appropriable rents, and the competitive contracting process, Journal of Law and Economics 21:2 (1978) 297-326.

28 Klein, B.H., Dynamic Economics (Harvard University Press, Cambridge, 1977).

29 Knight, F.H., Risk, Uncertainty, and Profit (University of Chicago Press, Chicago, 1971 [first published in 1921]).

30 Koopmans, T., Three Essays on the State of Economic Science (McGraw-Hill, New York, 1957).

31 Langlois, R.N., Why Are There Firms, Discussion paper 81-30, C.V. Starr Center for Applied Economics, New York Univ. (1981).

32 Langlois, R.N., Economics as a Process: Notes on the 'New Institutional Economics, Research Report 82-21, C.V. Starr Center for Applied Economics, New York Univ. (1982a).

33 Langlois, R.N., Subjective Probability and Subjective Economics, Research Report 82-09, C.V. Starr Center for Applied Economics, New York Univ. (1982b).

34 Langlois, R.N., Systems theory, knowledge, and the social sciences, in: Machlup, F. and Mansfield, U. (eds.), The Study of Information: Interdisciplinary Messages (John Wiley, New York, 1983).

35 Loasby, B., Choice, Complexity, and Ignorance (Cambridge University Press, Cambridge, 1976).

36 Machlup, F., Epilogue: semantic quirks in studies of information, in: Machlup, F. and Mansfield, U. (eds.), The Study of Information: Interdisciplinary Messages (John Wiley, New York, 1983).

37 Marschak, J. and Radner, R., The Economic Theory of Teams (Yale University Press, New Haven, 1972).

38 Monteverde, K. and Teece, D., Appropriable rents and quasi-vertical integration, Journal of Law and Economics 25:2 (1982a) 321-328.

39 Monteverde, K. and Teece, D., Supplier switching costs and vertical integration in the automobile industry, Bell Journal of Economics 13:1 (1982b) 206-213.

40 Nelson, R.R. and Winter, S.G., An Evolutionary Theory of Economic Change (Harvard University Press, Cambridge, 1982).

41 O'Driscoll, G.P. and Rizzo, M.J., The Economics of Time and Ignorance (Basil Blackwell, Oxford, 1984).

42 Polanyi, M., Personal Knowledge (University of Chicago Press, Chicago, 1958).

43 Posner, R., Economic Analysis of Law, second edition (Little-Brown, Boston, 1977).

44 Schon, D., Beyond the Stable State (Temple Smith, London, 1971).

45 Schotter, A., The Economic Theory of Social Institutions (Cambridge University Press, New York, 1981).

46 Schumpeter, J.A., The Theory of Economic Development (Harvard University Press, Cambridge, 1934; Oxford University Press, New York, 1961).

47 Schumpeter, J.A., Capitalism, Socialism, and Democracy (Harper and Brothers, New York, 1942; Harper Colophon edition, 1976).

48 Scriven, M., Explanation and prediction in evolutionary theory, Science 130 (1959) 447-482.

49 Shackle, G.L.S., Epistemics and Economics (Cambridge University Press, Cambridge, 1972).

50 Simon, H.A., Rationality as process and as product of thought, American Economic Review 68:2 (1978) 4.

51 Stigler, G., The division of labor is limited by the extent of the market, Journal of Political Economy 59:3 (1951), reprinted in: The Organization of Industry ch. 12 (Richard D. Irwin, Homewood, 1968).

52 Teece, D., Economies of scope and the scope of the enterprise, Journal of Economic Behavior and Organization 1:3 (1980) 223.

53 Teece, D., Some Efficiency Properties of the Modern Corporation: Theory and Evidence, manuscript, Stanford Univ. (1982a).

54 Teece, D., Towards an economic theory of the multiproduct firm, Journal of Economic Behavior and Organization 3 (1982b) 39-63.

55 Ullmann-Margalit, E., Invisible hand explanations, Synthese 39 (1978) 282-286.

56 Von Mises, L., Human Action (Yale University Press, New Haven, 1949).

57 Williamson, O.E., Markets and Hierarchies: Analysis and Antitrust Implications (The Free Press, New York, 1975).

58 Williamson, O.E., Transaction cost economics: the governance of contractual relations, Journal of Law and Economics 22:2 (1979) 233-261.

59 Williamson, O.E., The organization of work: a comparative institutional assessment, Journal of Economic Behavior and Organization 1:1 (1980) 5-38.

60 Williamson, O.E., The modern corporation: origin, evolution, attributes, Journal of Economic Literature 19 (1981) 1537.

61 Winter, S., Economic 'natural selection' and the theory of the firm, Yale Economic Essays 4 (1964) 225-272.

62 Winter, S., Optimization and evolution in the theory of the firm, in: Day, R. and Groves, T. (eds.), Adaptive Economic Models (Academic Press, New York, 1975).

COMMUNICATION AND INFORMATION ECONOMICS:
New Perspectives
M. Jussawalla and H. Ebenfield (Editors)

INTERNATIONAL TRADE AND INFORMATION: SOME WELFARE IMPLICATIONS

Meheroo Jussawalla and Chee-Wah Cheah

INTRODUCTION

Rapid advances in communication technology have rendered the accounting of an information sector a very real component of the traditional social accounting system of post-industrial society. Increasing recognition is being given to the allocation of information as a primary resource. International trade is no longer composed only of the output of agriculture and manufacturing but also of the services that take care of information flows between countries and the channels that carry this information. Transfer of communication technology from industrialized to developing countries influences the allocation of financial and material resources that are used to meet requirements of the balance of payments. Information can be treated both as a commodity and as a resource. In the latter category it has the advantage of being a renewable resource that also suffers from a high rate of obsolescence. As information technology, science, and research get more innovative, information that is traded has to be constantly revised. The advantage of trade in information goods and services appears to be innovative communication technology which enables trade and transfer at lower unit costs.

Marschak (1971) claimed that economists cannot deny that "a large part of our national product is contributed by symbol manipulation." What economists need to determine is the demand and supply of those goods and services used to manipulate symbols. Only then does it become possible to understand how social welfare is affected by resource allocation to such symbol-manipulating goods and services. The welfare effects of the communication revolution upon society need to be carefully assessed. As the interface between satellites and computers grows and as computer-to-computer communications become more widespread, both developed and developing countries will find their economic growth determined increasingly by investment in innovative information technology. Although we cannot predict the final outcome of the developments taking place, we can identify some of the possibilities for international trade and anticipate the trends for future welfare.

Trade flows are not strictly comparable to information flows, but the latter influence and formulate changes in elasticity of demand for certain products and services in both international capital markets and consumer markets, even though the quality and reliability of information generates differences in such elasticity. For example, electronic funds transfer, the transmission of arbitrage transactions, and currency rate fluctuations are so rapid that the economic distance between countries is increasingly determined by the quality of the data, the quality of the media, and the availability of communication and consultancy services.

Information technology has introduced a technological dependence and a technology gap between countries that threatens to distort the existing pattern of international trade--perhaps to make it worse for the developing world. While developing countries are trying to catch up with their industrialization and reach the target set at Lima in 1976 to supply 25 percent of the world's manufactured goods by 1990, this advantage is eroded as innovative technology reinforces the lead of more developed countries. Specialized resources of information skills and physical equipment for storage and retrieval are concentrated in the advanced countries, which makes it cost effective for less developed countries (LDCs) to import information technology. From the availability point of view, trade theory is a more rational approach; from the point of view of economic development and social welfare, the perpetration of the information gap constitutes a new form of colonialism which LDCs resent.

This paper examines information flows as an integral part of international trade, their impact on trade theory, and the implications for welfare. Since information is likely to enter the production function, questions of access to information and control and regulation of information flows become paramount in view of their consequences for the existing socioeconomic order. Trade in information is germane to national security, commerce, and technology transfer. It is not the intent of the authors to comment on the wide range of noneconomic issues like privacy, political freedom, cultural identity, and national sovereignty. Rather, our purpose is to deal with the less discussed and less familiar economic issues as distinct from those that are sociocultural in nature. It is an incomplete approach to the conceptualization of information flows traded across national borders as an economic problem. It indicates the areas in which research ought to be extended to provide policy guidelines. Included in this paper is an attempt to apply the technology theory of trade to transborder data flows (TBDF).

TRADE THEORY AND INFORMATION

Traditional neoclassical economic theory stipulates the efficiency of resource allocation engendered by spontaneous functioning of competitive markets based on the Paretian assumption that initial distribution of assets and income is given and unchangeable. However, the literature of economics has developed a powerful case against markets as guarantors of efficiency even in the theory of pure competition (Helleiner 1978). This is specially true of international markets because they are influenced by political and social systems. Political decisions often determine which markets can operate and which are repressed (Diaz-Alejandro 1976). Conventional wisdom dictates that economic relationships between countries ought to depend upon the terms of trade and the patterns of exchange between them. Heckscher and Ohlin stipulated factor abundance and factor intensity as determinants of specialization. The pattern of trade depends on pretrade prices, and it is assumed that free trade and specialization will bring about factor-price equalization, which is expected to eliminate international differences in incomes paid to the factors of production. It was assumed in the Heckscher-Ohlin theorem that factor abundance was determined by prices and that there was international identity of production functions and non-reversibility of factor intensities. But the theorem essentially explained the pattern of trade rather than trade efficiency. This analysis was extended by Ohlin (1967) to interregional trade with the use of location theory in which arguments are advanced to explain the relationship between obstacles to movement of commodities and the location of production. According to Ohlim, "not only the supply of productive factors in each country but also its local distribution and the relative transferability of goods is relevant." In this static framework of comparative advantage there was no indication of how changes in the conditions of production or changes in the input of knowledge into these conditions will affect the variables in the trade models. So far, the main assumption of factor immobility has been tacitly observed for flows between countries, but factors are assumed to be fully mobile within each country. As long as both countries are incompletely specialized, trade will lead to factor-price equalization. As factor endowments differ more and more between two trading partners, there will be complete specialization, in which case complete factor-price equalization will not occur. In the framework of such a static traditional theory of international trade, we have to introduce dynamic variables of technical change and the increasing input of knowledge and information into the production process to the extent that it is now possible to claim that information can be treated as a component of the production function (Torr 1980). As communication technology becomes increasingly innovative, the input of information becomes more important in terms of volume and value of the final product or output. In other words, information and knowledge become prime movers of technical change.

The influence of technical change on trade is not confined to its direct effects on comparative cost ratios; instead it may affect trade directly through its impact on economic growth, and changes in comparative cost may follow as an indirect response to price changes (Johnson 1963). Any improvement or reduction in cost of international communications will have a trade-increasing effect. At the same time, it is possible for communication technology to create trade limitations by generating barriers in the form of protection to the profits emerging from innovative technology. Trade policy may move in the direction of promoting internal rather than international trade if domestic profits are higher than gains from trade.

It is important in this context to note that rapid advances in communication technology have made it possible to transmit knowledge from one country to another, giving rise to technical change in the knowledge-importing country. The benefits of such transmission to the recipient country will be determined by the gains from increased productivity depending on the terms of trade for receiving the transmitted knowledge for technical change. In developing countries, the application of communication technology may have either an import-biased effect when transnational corporations (TNC) establish subsidiaries to supply the market of the developing country, or an export-biased effect when a subsidiary is established to supply goods to the home market where the TNC is headquartered. It therefore becomes difficult to separate trade caused by differences in technical knowledge from trade caused by differences in factor endowment (Posner 1961). If there is a continued supply of new and innovative information as a result of research and development in any one country or region, then this rate of information processing and transmission will be closely linked to a higher rate of net investment. With instant communication of science and technology between industrially advanced and developing countries the learning period tends to be reduced. This is especially so in instances when off-the-shelf technology is imported by developing countries. The lesser the degree of competition for the information technology or its product the greater will be the economic reaction lag, i.e., the investment time-lag for adaptation or imitation.

The separation of national markets gives rise to a demand lag in international trade as a response to competition in the supply of an information-intensive output. This applies in general to all imported technical change but is more marked in commodities like computers, videotape records, and such other goods imported by developing countries. These lags are removed when the domestic economy produces its own information goods and services at lower costs and access to them becomes affordable in the domestic market.

It becomes fairly apparent that, theoretically speaking, free trade and specialization tend to bring about factor-price equalization. According to Samuelson (1948), if knowledge were completely mobile and production functions were the same in all countries, then factor prices would be equalized through trade under certain conditions. The factor-price equalization model then became "the cornerstone of international trade theory," as Baldwin (1970) asserts. While transportation costs have generally been considered relevant in trade theory, information costs as a part of the costs of transferring inputs and outputs have been considerably ignored. The costs of information gathering to make trade possible are generally high and need to be reckoned. They vary among products and factors like other production costs. The degree of risk and uncertainty prevailing in foreign markets adds to the cost of obtaining information to reduce these risks for trade in goods and services. The higher the degree of risk and uncertainty, the higher the demand for information inputs. As communication technology tends to reduce the costs of obtaining information about investment and exchange prospects, larger corporations avail themselves of the benefits because they are equipped to transfer technological knowledge to subsidiary firms in developing countries. The costs of transferring inputs and outputs among countries are constantly reduced by advances in communication technology, which reduces the need for high costs of transportation by such devices as computer-to-computer communications assisted through geostationary satellites. Not only do input and output flows of information change the pattern of trade, but the very composition of trade flows is rapidly changing. As will shown later, the overall balance of payments of the industrially advanced countries, now classified as information economies, are more influenced by trade in services than by trade in merchandise. It may be possible to ascertain what percentage of this services trade can be ascribed to trade in information services and transborder data flows (TBDF).

TRADE THEORY, INFORMATION AND DEVELOPMENT

Some of the explicit assumptions of trade theory which lead to the proposition that free trade will solve the problems of development stand challenged in the context of demands made by developing countries for a more equitable economic order. Kitamura (1968) has criticized the weakness of the static assumptions of trade theory regarding fixed factor proportions and has argued that with technical progress, free trade does not maximize the welfare of less developed countries. Unless factors of production are consciously guided in their transfer, there is no inherent tendency to equalize factor incomes and productivity levels.

As information-intensive industries now feature extensively in international trade flows, the terms of trade are affected because of the impact of information on the marginal productivity of both labor and capital. Since information renders the production process either labor-saving, capital-saving, or neutral, communication technology enters to alter the marginal productivity of production factors in developing countries, inducing exports of information-intensive commodities. The ratio of productivity to wages is higher in developed countries because information input leading to skill formation is higher. Capital flows to those countries that have high productivity-to-wage ratios, thereby increasing the technology gap and the wage differentials. Prebisch (1959) challenged this assumption of higher productivity and the competitive nature of factor and product markets. Increased productivity does not lead to lower prices for the exports to periphery countries characterized by adverse terms of trade for their primary product exports and their capital equipment imports. Therefore, if free trade is unable to increase the relative information endowment of developing countries, conscious decisions will have to be taken by policy-makers to direct information to LDCs through aid, technical assistance, and preferential trade agreements. If conventional wisdom is to be followed, then favorable terms for information transfer should provide the basis for development of the Third World in such a way that improved international division of labor gets adjusted to factor endowments (Samir Amin 1979).

In his paper on availability, Kravis (1956) claimed that differences in relative wages are not the controlling factor for the composition of trade but that differences in relative output per worker are significant. According to the availability doctrine, the demand for imports of capital-intensive products is generated by the lack of their availability in the domestic markets of developing countries. We now find that technological change in the communication industry has caused information-intensive commodities and services to have a low import elasticity of demand in LDCs. Every developing country wants to improve the relative efficiency of its domestic industries by taking advantage of greater information-intensity that results in higher productivity. When international differences in productivity are not proportionately offset by differences in wages, then the cause of trade will be productivity differentials rather than wage differentials. The absence of complete free trade and free competition tends to limit trade to those commodities that are not produced in the importing developing country. In this context, communication hardware and software, e.g., satellites, computers, digital telephone systems, optical fiber networks, microprocessors, and their programming are currently being extensively imported by developing countries. As technology continues to reduce the costs of these imports, LDCs find the options cost-effective and the opportunity costs affordable, thereby making telecommunications infrastructure a determinant of economic development.

However, in a real world situation, international trade theory and its explanation of the composition and terms of trade fail to operate either on the basis of factor abundance or on the basis of availability, because of the sphere of control of transnational corporations (TNCs) based in industrially advanced countries. Magdoff (1976) estimated that the internal capital accumulation of TNCs is generating output in host countries that exceeds the total volume of international trade. This implies that international trade is no longer the main vehicle of international exchange of goods and services. Acquisition of bases in the developing world facilitates penetration of global markets by oligopolistic corporations that create barriers to entry by the use of exclusive information networks and vertical integration of the stages of production.

In theory, direct foreign investment is treated as the export of surplus capital from industrialized countries seeking higher rates of return. But with rigidly high interest rates currently prevailing in these countries, the dynamics of expansion are no longer tied to high rates of return. Activities of TNCs are more part of an organizational structure resulting in a new division of labor. There is mutually penetrating investment among TNCs with access to transnational banking and crucial data bases, which give them greater dominance in the flow of communication technology. Developing countries have to safeguard their balance of payments from such adverse consequences as repatriation of foreign capital, transfer of profits and dividends from host countries, and payments for technology imports. The hidden costs of technology transfer by TNCs are high due to the transfer pricing techniques they use. Royalties and service fees add to the burden of imported technology. Magee (1977) argues that TNCs deliberately use sophisticated technology in producing and transmitting information so that they can appropriate returns on it. Schiller's analysis (1981) supports this hypothesis because he provides empirical evidence to show the control of American TNCs over global distribution of information technology and the hidden costs involved for acquiring it. TNCs replace the market in trade and operate non-market systems for exports. Therefore, in the real world theoretical conditions for Pareto optimality through international trade are difficult to fulfill.

Market imperfections for information goods and services are not only characterized by oligopoly but by the information available to "arms length" purchasers and the high costs of search. The purchase of any technology involves the high cost of search. Quasi rent rises because the marginal cost to the owner declines with further information about the technology in question. Developing countries are learning to cope with these market imperfections by seeking reforms in the World Intellectual Property Organization to enable greater competition and to place obligations on those who own property rights to extend their use in developing countries.

Such impediments to trade in information have brought forth a new form of reprisal from LDCs in the form of "countertrade." According to *Business Week* (July 19, 1982), countertrade transactions constitute 25 to 30 percent of total world trade as developing countries attempt to narrow their balance-of-payments deficits. For example, Brazil has commissioned a communication satellite from Canada's Spar Aerospace jointly with Hughes Aircraft. Under the contract, these two companies will have to arrange for $130 million worth of Brazilian imports into Canada. As more barter arrangements become mandatory and widespread, the free market will be restricted. The flow of technology to LDCs may be reduced to the extent that industrialized countries will be required to export markets as substitutes for the export of credit. This will generate a trade-limiting effect and may prove counterproductive for the Third World in the long term.

Even if international trade makes a significant contribution to increases in GNP, apart from the foreign trade multiplier effects, there is no guarantee that an equitable distribution of gains from trade will take place. While the slogan "trade not aid" has been propagated by the developing world, the problem it faces is what the composition of trade should be to render its balances favorable for development. It is in this area that the information industries in general and microelectronics in particular have supported development-oriented trade. Export processing zones have operated for the semiconductor industry in Southeast Asia, resulting in higher employment and labor-intensive output. It is relevant here to note that it may have been futile for LDCs to have pushed their factors of production into traditional export activities or even into import substitution since price elasticity is low for such output and this tends to worsen the terms of trade, as pointed out by Bhagwati (1958) in his theory of immiserizing growth. However, in the microelectronics industry, the convergence of such components as computers and telecommunications makes possible the economic availability of a coherent system of information processing and distribution. This trend substantially alters the theory of comparative advantage inasmuch as the advantage is now man-made and introduced through the mastery of science and technology (Rada 1981). As information-intensive industries become more widespread, there is a further polarization in the international division of labor. This is because of the concentration of research and development (R&D) in the industrialized countries. The United States controls about 90 percent of the computer market and service networks worldwide.

Table 1

Mainframe Computer Market, 1979
(Share of the market based on the value of total units installed)

Company	Percent
IBM	64.3
Honeywell	8.7
Sperry Rand-Univac	8.0
Burroughs	6.4
Control Data	4.1
NCR	1.9
Others	6.6

Source: Quantum Science Corporation 1979

Concentration in this sector has strengthened since U.S. computer companies' revenues have increased from $12.2 billion in 1972 to $53.3 billion in 1980, in which year IBM's share was 49 percent. Similar concentration exists in software and machine services and data banks. The United States has 49 percent of data bases and holds 64 percent of records worldwide.

The accumulating factor in this case is information intensity. Trade theory postulates that factor growth leads to a deterioration in the terms of trade for that commodity or service that uses the accumulating factor intensively given other conditions, like commodity prices, factor prices, and homogeneous production functions, are constant. According to this hypothesis, when the accumulating factor (information) is used intensively in the export industry, the effects on the growth of national income may not be fully positive. This is particularly so if the share of exports in national income is large because theory assumes that the terms of trade will go against the exporting country (Rybczynski 1955). However, this aspect of trade theory cannot be substantiated in the context of the changes in information technology that enable intensive application of microelectronics to many spheres of production. Low price elasticity of demand for the output of office equipment, photocopying, home computers, and earth stations for receiving satellite transmissions neutralizes the

Table 2

Reference Data Bases and Data-Base Records Distribution

Area	Year		
	1975	1977	1979
United States:			
Number of Data Bases	177	208	259
Number of Records (million)	46	58	94
Other Developed Market Economies:			
Number of Data Bases	124	154	269
Number of Records (million)	6	13	55

Source: ASIS Bulletin No. 7, December 1980, 27-29.

negative effects of factor accumulation and intensity. Japan, Western Europe, and the United States are all offering new exportables in communication and information processing commodities and services to their trading partners, and changes in demand patterns render the terms of trade favorable and improve the marginal productivity of labor along with the real wage of workers in the information industry.

This availability of information technology will not be detrimental to Third World development insofar as it opens up greater trade opportunities for them. For example, Asian countries such as Singapore, Hong Kong, South Korea, Malaysia, and Taiwan pursued outward looking trade policies and benefited from the microelectronics revolution and assembly and export of semiconductors. However, not all LDCs have promising export prospects, but, as Kravis (1970) argues, this may be due to deficiencies in supply conditions within developing countries rather than deficiency in export demand. The total impact of the Generalized System of Preferences (GSP) schemes has been limited and spread unevenly among the LDCs. So far as the information-based industries are concerned, the immediate benefits have accrued mainly to a small group of the newly industrializing countries which dominate LDC exports such as Taiwan, Mexico, Yugoslavia, South Korea, Hong Kong, Brazil, Singapore, and India. The electronics industry has used free trade zones in many of these countries for assembling and wiring of chips. However, automation in information-related output has reduced the importance of direct labor costs in total production costs. There is a shift of skill requirements for software based on systems engineering skills. Due to such automation, industrialized countries are not relying on their offshore installations to the same extent because automation minimizes labor costs, increases efficiency, and maintains employment levels within the domestic economy. The competitive capacity of low-labor-cost installations, is being eroded by high technology in developed countries. There is a transition of the industry to research and development in software. This will involve a change in development strategy in terms of productive infrastructure. The convergence of electronics with other industries will compel the Third World to move into new skill requirements and obtain the advantage of providing cheaper software, program analysis, and other intellectual skills that high technology demands.

A TECHNOLOGY THEORY OF TRADE: THE CASE OF TBDF

We start on the premise that technology is not universally available. Production functions are not identical in all countries. Hence, the basic feature determining a country's ability to participate in the market for computer communication services is the availability of technology, including that embodied in physical and human capital.[1] We assume that the ability to exploit the new technology of computer communications lies in the North. As a result, the North produces and exports new "products" which are primarily services in data processing, retrieval, and storage. Trade in these services constitute TBDF. It is also assumed that the North has the initial monopoly in the international computer communications industry. The monopoly rents accruing to the North account for the higher wages paid to Northern labor.

The flow of computer-generated information over time is determined by two processes of technological change, namely, innovation and technology transfer.[2] The factors affecting the rate of innovation in the North are not well known. But Vernon (1966) suggests that such factors may include the presence of a skilled labor force, external economies, or simply the existence of an appropriate "social atmosphere." With regards to the latter, it may be useful to think of innovation as being technical improvements generated in response to rising standards of living and changing relative costs of capital and labor. We will abstract from the exact determinants of innovation and assume that it takes place continually in the North.[3]

The analytical framework for technology transfer has a richer theoretical foundation. According to the innovation/imitation approach of Posner (1961) and Hufbauer (1965), there is a gradual transfer of technical improvements from the North to the South, where they could be applied more cheaply than in their country of origin. Low wages are often cited as the incentive for such transfers thereby converting "technological gap" trade into the familiar Heckscher-Ohlin trade based on differences in comparative advantage associated with differing factor endowments. It should be noted that differences in relative costs of human labor are essentially the results of differences in embodied human capital as well as of the immobility of labor.

To explain "technological gap" trade, we need a dynamic theory of comparative cost that provides the mechanisms of production transfer from the North to the South. According to Posner, such transfers may occur through successful imitation of the North's innovation by domestic producers in the South. In the case of TBDF (or for that matter, any other new product), this may require large investments in developing the requisite scientific and technical knowledge base for the viable operation of a domestic computer communication industry. Such investments in a competent Galbraithian "technostructure" may be riskily expensive both in terms of the amount of resources that have to be committed and the period for which they have to be committed. Although private investments may be motivated by potentially low capital costs, the socially optimum amount of investment may well require additional incentives in the form of economic protection.

Innovating firms, motivated by the prospect of imitation by domestic competitors, may also choose to transfer technology by direct foreign investment or by leasing their technology in return for royalties or profit shares. The choice between these two alternatives will depend on such factors as the competitive advantage of the innovating firm in research and development (R&D) or production and sales, as well as whether the R&D consists of a once-and-for-all development of a special purpose product or a continuous stream of improvements in the product. Within a Magee-type industry cycle, R&D investments and product and process differentiation should be high early in the industry's life cycle (Magee 1977). As such, firms engaged in computer communications will presumably have the competitive advantage in R&D that leads to a continuous stream of service innovation. Technology transfer in this instance will be characterized by the "internationalization of production." However, Vernon notes that investment decisions of this type are often made in the face of uncertain production conditions, factor prices, and availabilities in the host country. The result may be a delayed transfer of production beyond that which is economically efficient. Moreover, the transplantation of an industrial structure and way of doing business from the North to the South is not necessarily the most efficient procedure for developing the latter's economy.

Finally, technology may be transferred through the embodiment of knowledge either in material capital goods or in human capital. While this mechanism has the advantage in that the technology-borrowing South need not allocate resources to R&D investments, nor pay for technology in the form of profits or royalties, it entails the possibility of excessive payments for monopolized knowledge during the initial import phase. Even if the mechanism works, there may possibly be a very long lag before production actually gravitates to the South in accordance with shifting comparative advantage based on low wages.

Regardless of the manner in which computer communications technology is transferred, the relocation of production operates rather imperfectly with considerable lags. This is due as much to existing barriers in the international movement of data flows as to the special features of investments in knowledge production and in the creation of human capital. The picture of the world that we have painted can be summarized as follows. Firms engaged in computer communication services are constantly emerging in the North. These firms are characterized by large R&D investments, small optimum size, highly differentiated services, and diverse production processes as per Magee's industry cycle. Northern firms have the initial monopoly in computer communication services. Their monopoly power gets eroded by the diffusion of technology through the world economy in response to economic incentives provided by differences in relative labor costs. Thus, some Northern firms will disappear in the face of low-wage competition. This is in itself a "desirable" event from the view of world productive efficiency.

From a long-run efficiency standpoint, it is apparent that innovation represents an increase in real world productivity by increasing the range of services that are offered. Moreover, since technology transfers allow for an expansion of the production possibilities of the South, they also represent a welfare gain from a global point of view.[4] But with the incomes of Northern labor depending on the rents from their monopoly of new services, successful technological borrowing by the South will make the North worse off. As such, the North must continually innovate to maintain its welfare as well as the technological gap that enables trade in the first instance.

So far, we have ignored the costs of acquiring the technology by the South. Unless the factors that determine the rate of technological transfer are known, the implication of these costs for policy are unclear. However, it is clear that Southern protectionist policies may be self-defeating as they would delay the transfer of technology as dictated by production cost differentials. This delay may well add to the social costs of the eventual acquisition of the technology.

It is often tempting to policymakers that international differences in computer communication capabilities can be bridged by relatively small public investments. Such notions overlook the productive capacity of the South given its resource endowments. The contemporary policy emphasis on the importance to national economic prosperity of controlling TBDF is merely a sophisticated translation of the hoary infant industry argument for protection. If trade in computer communication services that lead to TBDF is the outcome of a North-South technological gap, then the existing trade flows are a manifestation of a dynamic disequilibrium in the spread of awareness and exploitation of new economic opportunities. This disequilibrium is continually being renewed by innovation in the North and eroded by diffusion of technology to the South. We may find comfort in the fact that even in the poorest countries one now finds computers in use, although the widespread commercial applications of computers in the advanced countries are only 30 years or so old.

INFORMATION PRODUCTS IN INTERNATIONAL TRADE AND TRANSBORDER DATA FLOWS

A study of the United States information trade (Rubin and Sapp 1981) found that the information sector has consistently produced a favorable balance of payments. In 1965 the favorable balance was $1.7 billion, and this figure rose to $8.9 billion by 1978. During this period, other sectors of the U.S. economy also had a positive trade balance. Over the period of the study (1965-1978), the contribution of information-related exports to GNP was one-half of 1 percent, but it must be noted that imports grew equally rapidly and cancelled out the increase in exports. However, the percentage of sales overseas of U.S. leading exporters of information-related hardware has increased since 1978 despite the escalation in the international value of the dollar during the years 1980-82. It has been estimated that each percentage point increase in the value of the dollar costs the United States $3 billion in net exports (Fortune, August 9, 1982). Despite this burden, leading exporters in information goods have a high percentage of export sales as a proportion of total sales. Information hardware exports by ten companies who rank among the Fortune 500 show trends of high exports.

In this area of information-related trade, data flows via electronic transmission have become significant incumbent upon the merger of computers with telecommunications. From a technical point of view, transborder data flows (TBDF) are movements of data across national boundaries for the purposes of processing storage and retrieval. For this paper, TBDF are those flows consequent on contractual relationships between parties in two or more countries. Only in recent years have nations become aware of their economic and social implications.

The problem of TBDF in a changing world order has been further complicated by the infusion of competing national interests based on claims (either real or hypothetical) of data/technology dependencies and domination. These flows have clearly evoked a whole set of national sentiments that are overly sensitive to areas like data privacy and data piracy and internat-

Table 3

Growing Share of Information Sector in Exports

Rank		Company	Products	Total Exports as Percent of Sales
'81	'80			
9	9	IBM	Information handling systems, equipment	6.39
11	13	Westinghouse	Generating equipment and Defense systems	14.00
12	19	Signal Companies	Trucks, engines, audio-video systems	22.81
17	19	Hewlett Packard	Electronic equipment	27.14
29	38	Digital Equipment	Computer systems	21.42
'80	'81			
36	35	Rockwell International	Electronic, automotive, and industrial equipment	7.51
37	39	Sperry	Computer systems and equipment	9.45
45	48	Minnesota Mining and Manufacturing	Industrial, health care, graphics, electronics products	6.52
47	47	Control Data	Computers and equipment	13.29
50	45	Emerson Electric	Electronic components	20.59

Source: Fortune, August 9, 1982

ional relations in general. In fact, protectionist policies on TBDF have either been proposed or adopted by certain countries, e.g., Brazil. Based essentially on past practices in the trade of conventional goods and services, the relevance and appropriateness of such policies are perhaps premature because of the complexities of data flows where no accounting standards as yet exist. Lacking precise measurements of data volume, these policies may amount to an imposition of invisible barriers to invisible exchanges. A careful consideration of trade in data flows should include those complementary values relating to gains and opportunities arising from mutually beneficial exchange.

It is evidently clear that some current debates over TBDF (and the principle of free flow) are based on real concerns with economic undertones. However, they need to be separated from the milieu of sociopolitical issues that now encumber a precise understanding of the TBDF problem in economic terms. Only then can we begin to develop a concerted approach for analyzing trade policies as they apply to such flows. Whether or not allusions about the impact of TBDF on economic growth and development are real or imagined remains an empirical question. Our purpose here is to present an exploratory and tentative assessment of the economic dimensions of data flows.

We proceed on the premise that some aspects of TBDF acquire new meanings when they are considered in terms of the informational and organizational features of economic trade and exchange. For instance, it is becoming more apparent that the relevant economic distance between nations hinges on factors such as the quality of data received or transmitted, the quality of existing communication media, and the availability of communication channels together with supporting services (Jussawalla 1982). Thus, the efficiency of international markets will depend on access to communication channels and informational resources as much as on a priori differences in information endowments.

Recent works in economic theory have demonstrated that informational problems caused market failures of various kinds. Interesting results are obtained from extensions of these ideas to the micro theory of the firm. It has long been maintained that the chief rationale of the firm is its organizational role in economizing on transactions costs (Coase 1937). As such, the firm has a choice of exchange modes for resource allocation purposes, viz., exchange via market mediated processes or internal contracting by means of team production. Given that "resources needed to obtain information may be independent of the scale of the production process in which the information is used" (Radner 1970), market contracting may inhibit the firm's allocative efficiency of information-exchange between successive stages of production. This is because of contractual problems related to specification and enforcement of contract terms. Thus, the firm can be subjected to "organizational failures" traceable to informational problems (Williamson 1975).

While this concept applies to firms operating at the domestic level, we submit that it is also true for firms operating in world markets with informational problems perhaps exacerbated by greater market uncertainties and complexities. Consequently, information acquisition via market channels gets replaced by vertical integration with information flows internalized by the establishment of transnational corporations. TBDF involving movements of operational data which support organization decision-making and administrative functions are examples of such flows. From an organizational standpoint, TBDF are essentially manifestations of institutional responses to problems of resource allocation within an informationally constrained environment. Yet, national perceptions about unrestricted data flows associated with the operations of multinational activities are somewhat negative. The tendency towards government control of such data flows is not completely explicable on economic grounds.

Recent attempts to exercise greater control over multinational activities, data importation and exportation by certain countries can be interpreted as institutional rearrangements relating to the market for TBDF. Granted that these institutional changes may eventually alter the pattern of data flows between nations, we should not ignore the fact that such changes are themselves resource-using activities. Proposals for complete equality of access to informational resources may entail arrangements that cannot be feasibly implemented or are too costly to enforce. In a "second-best" world where transaction costs abound, the relevant efficiency principle is one based on minimization of excess burden (Demsetz 1972). Thus, comparisons between a real and an ideal situation are not only inappropriate, they tend to result in misleading claims with no proper economic rationale.

Concerns over uneven data flows are magnified especially for those nations whose industrial mix includes a disproportionate percentage of foreign-owned organizations. Aside from impacts on local industry and employment, the disproportionate amount of data outflow is perceived to be detrimental to a nation's security. Under these circumstances, national controls over data flows are rationalized on grounds of data vulnerability to possible misuse as foreign-located information is ultra vires of the home country's legal system. Abstracting from privacy "rights" for the moment, we suggest that TBDF involving personal data serves useful economic functions. Personal data are all potentially relevant market signals in a variety of markets. Put to proper use, these signals can affect resource allocation decisions which are consistent with changing market parameters. Moreover, these same signals can be used as filtering or screening devices particularly in transactions that involve large risks and uncertainty. Controls over personal data flows may thus amount to the creation of barriers inhibiting very ordinary functions of commercial enterprises.

On the other hand, we concede that personal data interpreted as market signals can be applied to influence and formulate changes in tastes and demand elasticity of certain goods and services. The phenomena of "demonstration effect" and "cultural dependence" cited in the development literature are critical references to this aspect of developed economies' role on the development process of LDCs. It is apparent that these impacts are no longer impeded by information and transportation costs. Thus, LDCs are quite rightly anxious in protecting themselves against the adversity of such imported alternatives. However, this must be balanced by other considerations. In an increasingly global society, exposure to foreign influences is inevitable for an open economy. Unless an economy consciously resorts to the improbable situation of autarky, it is not obvious that control over TBDF of personal information will alleviate the risk of loss of cultural identity. In a comparative institutional framework, ideological claims of "cultural dependence" must be tempered by an economic evaluation of alternatives that are real and possible.

From an economic perspective, we may view privacy rights as a broader conception of rights to property like land and other tangibles. Property rights serve an economic function insofar as they pertain to resource allocation by creating the appropriate incentives for putting resources into the highest valued use (Posner 1973). The guiding principle here is to assign property rights in such a manner that the value of data used for any particular purpose exceeds the cost of real or potential privacy intrusions. By granting individuals the right to withhold information or to exclude collection and usage of personal data about themselves, we can be assured that data will be divulged in a market transaction only if the value of so doing exceeds the cost of privacy impairment. It is in this sense that personal data will be allocated to its highest value use, once property rights are clearly defined.

However, the condition of exclusivity in property rights is clearly violated in the case of data flows. In particular, the right to exclude undue accessibility to data files or the right to exclude improper usage cannot be properly specified for various reasons, including differences in legal and cultural conceptions of privacy. There is a further economic reason. Suppose we can assign privacy rights by requiring individual consent prior to data dissemination or usage, the transaction costs resulting from multilateral contracting between a data vendor and a host of individuals would be formidable. It is apparent that such high transactions costs could impair the allocative efficiency of data usage by protecting privacy.

However, in the absence of any overarching international legal framework at the present moment, provisions to enforce privacy rights should be evaluated in terms of the economic incentives they pose for data flows. Failure to deter data misuse at the margin may lead to allocative inefficiencies and very often create knee-jerk reactions on the part of threatened nations.

WELFARE IMPLICATIONS OF INTERNATIONAL TRADE IN INFORMATION

Welfare propositions in international trade theory date back to Samuelson's (1939) analysis of the gains from trade and their distribution among countries. The measurement of welfare changes relate to the need of decision makers to formulate policy. It is not just the cost/benefit aspect of a trade policy that needs quantification for welfare, but as Bhagwati (1963) pointed out, there is the need to measure economic relationships and to ascertain which changes in the direction of trade policy are desirable for economic welfare. For national welfare, the proposition that free trade is better than no trade is in fact the welfare side of the theory of comparative advantage, satisfying standard "first best" conditions. When income distribution enters the calculus, it is possible to rank trade policy for tariffs. However, with information technology changing the composition and direction of trade, market distortions confound the standard "first best" condition. This is particularly true under conditions of oligopoly when production of computers, holding of data bases, and manufacturing and launching of satellites are all centered in a few First World countries. World welfare has to settle for second-best conditions like restricted trade being better than no trade. For developing countries, technology transfer through transnational corporations establishing subsidiaries in LDCs further distorts the free-trade criterion. As shown in the previous section, while communication technology is considered essential for the optimum utilization of information in the production process, most of this technology is centered in First World countries, so that LDCs have to import the hardware or the know-how of production to avail themselves of speedy, cost-efficient communications. However, the squeeze on Third World borrowers and the costs of borrowing have already laid a heavy debt burden on non-oil exporting LDCs, further reducing world welfare.

The validity of the welfare proposition of trade theory becomes questionable in the context of the expansion of information flows across national borders. Divergences in external economies arise because of the widening gap between information-rich and information-poor nations, divergences in wage-price ratios, and other characteristics of developing countries. For example, a divergence between private and social marginal rates of transformation arises in a developing country because of inadequate communication channels, which results in a lack of coordination between development agencies, the production sector, and trade policy. It is possible to import certain goods and services that can be produced cheaply in the domestic market because of insufficient communication channels within a developing country. In the context of development, the welfare propositions of trade theory get modified if information of the current period is treated as factor endowment of the following period. Can we calculate the net effect on real income of a change in information stock, irrespective of whether that change is autonomous or induced? If it can be calculated, then the welfare propositions of trade theory, viz., free trade is better than no trade and restricted trade is better than no trade, can be applied to information flows in the same manner as they are applied to the flows of merchandise and services. Even with restricted validity of the welfare assumptions, extending the welfare hypothesis to information flows does not yield a first-best solution because of divergence in external economies that are incompatible with the optimality of a perfectly competitive equilibrium. If we consider only the allocative part of the concept of welfare as distinct from any compensation factor (Little 1957), we still find that the welfare assumptions of trade theory do not provide the best allocative solution to the distribution of information or the best allocation of information resources. International comparisons of welfare are involved as a judgment of facts. But as Mishan (1981) argues, the notion of economic efficiency is, at base, a value judgment. It is just that the value judgment has to be rendered explicit.

Applying the welfare criteria to the real world system, we find that the share of developing countries in world trade in information goods (television, radio, computers, books, journals, telephone equipment) has been increasing as part of the value of world trade. Some of them have not reaped greater benefits from expanding world trade in information goods and services due to drawbacks in their domestic organizational structures and deficiency in demand for their products. There is widespread acceptance of the view that international trade has not worked to the advantage of the poor nations. This has led to an intensification of the demand at UNCTAD VI and at North-South Conferences by developing countries to reform the international trade system.

In like manner, Unesco meetings along with meetings of the International Telecommunications Union have been characterized by demands for a New World Communications/Information Order. Two international commissions (the Brandt Commission and the MacBride Commission) have separately dealt with these issues. Some trade liberalization measures plus special stabilization measures have been helpful to developing countries, especially to the newly industrialized countries, but have not led to substantial resource transfers. The success that some of them have enjoyed is as much the result of their own efforts as of the welfare effects of the trading system.

The middle-income developing countries have shifted away from import-substitution and adjusted their trade policies to the existing resource patterns within their domestic economies. Trade performance has been improving for outward-looking developing countries, which enables them to shift to more demanding, skill-intensive, and technology-intensive areas of production like information and communication products and services. The major difference between the low-income and middle-income LDCs, as noted in the World Development Report (1981), is not the structure but the amount of trade. The export to GNP ratio is three times larger for the middle-income countries.

Table 4

Structure of Merchandise Trade, Low- and Middle-income Oil Importers, 1970-80

Year, country group and region	Export-GDP ratio	Composition of merchandise exports (percentage)		Composition of merchandise imports (percentage)		
		Manufactures	Nonfuel primary	Manufactures	Food	Fuel
1970						
Low-income oil importers						
Africa	23	11	86	77	11	9
Asia	7	54	43	64	21	5
Middle-income oil importers	22	33	58	69	12	10
1980						
Low-income oil importers						
Africa	16	9	80	51	16	31
Asia	9	47	50	38	14	39
Middle-income oil importers	24	46	36	53	11	28

Source: World Bank (1981)

As the volume of developing country exports keeps increasing, their capacity to trade in information flows simultaneously increases with electronic funds transfer, telex and facsimile via satellite, and computer-to-computer networks, all facilitating information input into production and export activities. Their capacity to diversify has been demonstrated by their trade patterns, which means that they are able to offset the decline in terms of trade by gains in export receipts. Part of this welfare impact is attributable to South-South trade based on specialization among LDCs themselves. The low-income countries of Asia and Africa are still more dependent on growth in world demand due to their lower capacity to diversify their exports. There are several areas where the welfare hypothesis of trade theory has not been applicable. Trade in agricultural commodities is severely distorted by national price support and protection policies. But by far trade in services lacks an integrated system of international principles and conventions.

It is in the area of trade in services that information flows get included to a large extent. The World Bank (1981) reports that this sector generated one-third more revenue for developing countries in 1980 than did agricultural exports. More significant from the welfare point of view is whether the traditional approach to trade liberalization requires broadening in order to be more effective. The General Agreement on Tariffs and Trade (GATT) is based on the assumption that participating countries would have a higher benefit-to-cost ratio with open trade. But empirically these agreements have not brought participating countries to weigh all the benefits they derive from trade against costs. Countries continue to exclude products from tariff reductions, not because the producers' costs of lower tariffs would exceed the consumers' gains but because displaced producers can generate political pressures to resist liberalization. This is reflected in the safeguards and escape clauses introduced by industrialized countries in their trade negotiations with LDCs. Information trade is, therefore, likely to be severely restricted if such safeguards and escape clauses are introduced by the more developed countries. This will become more relevant as LDCs increase their share of world trade in information. Developing countries are called upon to reduce their import barriers despite escalating debt burdens, but they are unable to obtain matching concessions or reciprocity from industrial countries. Therefore the movement for countertrade is gathering momentum. With more subtle forms of non-tariff barriers and industry support programs, estimating the negative effects of protection on welfare implications for the developing world becomes a difficult task. There are trade action monitoring systems in the United States, Australia, and the Federal Republic of Germany which publish the costs of protection. But for data flows and information inputs, the sensitivity of services trade requires legislation to be worked into the decision-making institutions through which trade policy is administered. A whole new international regime is getting into place as information and communication technologies are assuming control of economic activities within countries and among trading partners.

NOTES

1 This is the view propounded by Kravis (1956) in his "availability" thesis.

2 Innovation is defined here as the process by which new services are created (by existing firms or new firms) consequent on the manner in which the existing software and hardware are improved and applied. See also note 3. Technology transfer refers to the process by which previously new services are transformed into "old" services which can now be produced in the South.

3 The usual models of trade based on "technological gaps" have the undesirable feature that trade ceases upon the successful imitation of the innovation by the South. This can be eliminated by employing the firm as the focal point in the analysis of new services. In reality, innovating firms not only channel a large portion of their resources toward innovation, they also provide continuity for the innovative process (see Harman 1971). Thus, innovation may be regarded as the development of new services and/or the increase in output of highly differentiated services as a result of either the internal growth of firms or increase in the number of firms.

4 A transfer of technology enables the substitution of Southern labor for Northern labor. Given the initial wage ratios, this would reduce production costs, thereby indicating that production possibilities of the South have expanded.

REFERENCES

1 Amin, Samir, NIEO: How to put Third World surpluses to effective use, Third World Quarterly 1:1 (January 1979).

2 Baldwin, R.E., International trade in inputs and outputs, in: Lamberton, D.M. (ed.), Economics of Information and Knowledge, 289-299 (Penguin, 1970).

3 Bhagwati, J., Immiserizing growth: A geometric note, Review of Economic Studies 25 (June 1958) 201-205.

4 Bhagwati, J., Some recent trends in the pure theory of international trade, in: Harrod, R.F. and Hague, D.C. (eds.), International Trade Theory in a Developing World, 22-30 (Macmillan, London, 1963).

5 Carlson, S., International transmission of information and the business firm, Annals of the American Academy of Political and Social Sciences 412 (1974) 55-63.

6 Coase, R.H., The nature of the firm, Economica 4 (1937) 386-405.

7 Demsetz, H., When does the rule of liability matter? Journal of Legal Studies 1:1 (1972) 13-28.

8 Diaz-Alejandro, C., North South relations: The economic component, International Organization 29:1 (1976) 213-241.

9 Harman, A.J., The International Computer Industry: Innovation and Comparative Advantage (Harvard University Press, Cambridge, 1971).

10 Hayek, F.H., The use of knowledge in society, American Economic Review 35 (1945) 519-30.

11 Helleiner, G., World market imperfections and the developing countries, Occasional Papers II, Overseas Development Council (U.S. Government Printing Office, Washington, D.C., 1978).

12 Hufbauer, G.C., Synthetic Materials and the Theory of International Trade (Duckworth, London, 1965).

13 Johnson, H.G., Effects of changes in comparative costs as influenced by technical change, in: Harrod, R.F. and Hague, D.C. (eds.), International Trade Theory in a Developing World (Macmillan, London, 1963).

14 Jussawalla, M., International trade theory and communication, in: Jussawalla, M. and Lamberton, D.M. (eds.), Communication Economics and Development, 92-99 (Pergamon Press, New York, 1982).

15 Kitamura, H., Capital accumulation and the theory of international trade, Malayan Economic Review 3:1 (1968). Reprinted in Livingstone (ed.), Economic Policy for Development (Penguin, 1971).

16 Kravis, I.B., Availability and other influences on commodity composition of trade, Journal of Political Economy 64 (April 1956) 143-155.

17 Kravis, I.B., Trade as a handmaiden of growth: Similarities between the nineteenth and twentieth centuries, Economic Journal 8 (1970) 850-872.

18 Little, I.M.D., A Critique of Welfare Economics, 2d ed. (Oxford University Press, 1957).

19 Magdoff, M., Multinational corporations and social development, in: Apte and Goodman (eds.), Multinational Corporations and Social Change, chapter 8 (Praeger, New York, 1976).

20 Magee, S., Information and the multinational corporation: An appropriability theory of direct foreign investment, in: Bhagwati, J. (ed.), The New International Economic Order: The North-South Debate, 318-337 (M.I.T. Press, Cambridge, 1977).

21 Marshack, Jacob, Economics of information systems, Journal of the American Statistical Association 66:33 (1971).

22 Mishan, E.J., Introduction to Normative Economics (Oxford University Press, New York, 1981).

23 Ohlin, Bertil, Interregional and International Trade (Harvard University Press, Cambridge, 1967).

24 Posner, M.V. [1961], International trade and technical change, in: Lamberton, D.M. (ed.), Economics of Information and Knowledge, 267-288 (Penguin, 1971).

25 Posner, R.A., Economic Analysis of Law (Little, Brown and Co., Boston, 1973).

26 Prebisch, R., Commercial policy in the underdeveloped countries, American Economic Review. Papers and Proceedings 49:2 (1959) 251.

27 Rada, Juan F., The microelectronics revolution: Implications for the Third World, Development Dialogue 2 (1981) 41-67.

28 Radner, R.A., Problems in the theory of markets under uncertainty, American Economic Review 60 (1970) 454-460.

29 Rubin, R.M. and Sapp, M.E., Selected roles of information in goods and services in the U.S. national economy, Information Processing and Management 17 (1981) 195-213.

30 Rybczynski, T.M., Factor endowment and relative commodity prices, Economica 22 (1955) 336-41.

31 Samuelson, P.A., The gains from international trade, Canadian Journal of Economics and Political Science 5 (1939) 195-205.

32 Samuelson, P.A., International trade and the equalisation of factor prices, Economic Journal 58 (1948) 163-184.

33 Schiller, H., Who Knows? Information in the Age of Fortune 500 (Ablex, Norwood, N.J., 1981).

34 Torr, C.S.W., The role of information in economic analysis, African Journal of Economics 48:2 (1980) 115-151.

35 Vernon, R., International investment and international trade in the product cycle, Quarterly Journal of Economics 80 (1966) 190-207.

36 Williamson, O.E., Markets and Hierarchies: Analysis and Antitrust Implications (Free Press, New York, 1975).

37 World Bank, World Development Report 1981 (Oxford University Press, New York, 1981).

COMMUNICATION AND INFORMATION ECONOMICS:
New Perspectives
M. Jussawalla and H. Ebenfield (Editors)

FEEDBACK MODELS: R&D, INFORMATION, AND PRODUCTIVITY GROWTH

William J. Baumol and Edward N. Wolff

Among the variables whose influence has frequently been tested in investigations of the productivity slowdown of the past two decades is expenditure on research and development. A first glance at the data seems to support the conclusion that during the period of decline in the rate of productivity growth (roughly, 1962-1980), R&D outlays for purposes other than defense and space exploration actually rose from 0.99 percent of GNP in 1963-64 to 1.11-1.13 percent in the period 1974-77. Yet there is apparently more to the matter. According to Rama (1980), in 1979, U.S. manufacturers expected their R&D budgets to equal less than 50 percent of their capital investment outlays compared to an 80 percent figure in the 1960s. And in 1975, private industry in the United States employed 6.1 percent fewer scientists and engineers than it did in 1970.[1] Here, then, is something to be explained. In a period of growing real GNP and of rising (nonmilitary) expenditures on R&D relative to GNP, why should there be a decline in both absolute and relative terms in number of engineers and scientists employed? And why the expected decline in R&D expenditures as compared to investment?

A second set of curious relationships also concerns us, for we will suggest that they stem from a source similar to that affecting the R&D outlays. It is generally agreed that productivity in the service sector has an inherent tendency to grow more slowly than it does in manufacturing and agriculture. A change in the shares of these two sectors in the composition of output is, therefore, frequently proposed as an explanation for part of the productivity slowdown. However, it has been argued that the ratio of the outputs of these two sectors has not changed materially (see Denison 1973, 1979). Yet, the proportion of the U.S. labor force employed in the service sector rose from 54 percent in 1948 to 64 percent in 1969.[2] Here, too, matters do not seem quite consistent. And, in any event, if a rise in the more stagnant sector's share of the labor force can be shown to be consistent with constancy of its share in output, one must still disentangle the implications for the economy's overall growth in productivity. Is one driven to the conclusion that the stagnant sector can bear no responsibility for the decline in productivity?

THE COST-DISEASE MODEL EXTENDED

Some years ago, one of us introduced a construct (Baumol 1967) that has since achieved a certain degree of notoriety and has been referred to as the cost-disease model or the unbalanced-growth model. In that model, the economy was taken to be composed of two sectors, a "progressive" sector, 1, in which productivity grows exponentially, and a stagnant sector, 2, in which productivity remains constant. There is a single input, labor, with quantities L_1 and L_2 used by the respective sectors, and whose outputs are given by

$$y_1 = c\, L_1 e^{rt} \qquad y_2 = d\, L_2. \tag{1}$$

Letting w represent the common wage rate, we have the unit cost figures

$$AC_1 = wL_1/y_1 = w/ce^{rt}\ , \quad AC_2 = wL_2/y_2 = w/d \tag{2}$$

or a relative cost for the stagnant sector which grows exponentially with time:

$$AC_2/AC_1 = ce^{rt}/d. \tag{3}$$

Thus we have

Proposition 1. In the cost-disease model, the per-unit cost of the output of the stagnant sector will rise without limit relative to that of the progressive sector.

This phenomenon has been referred to as the cost disease of the services (since Baumol associated a broad variety of services with stagnant sector 2).

Next, we introduce a third prototype type of output, one which, like our other two, is intended as an instructive special case which we call the asymptotically stagnant case. This third sector offers an activity that uses in (more or less) fixed proportions two different types of input, one deriving from progressive sector 1 and the other either deriving from stagnant sector 2 or being composed of pure labor (or some combination of the two).[3]

Two industries that seem to match this description most closely are television broadcasting (whose primary inputs are electronic equipment and live performance) and computer usage (whose main inputs are sophisticated hardware and human labor devoted to software creation).

On the assumption that input-output proportions are absolutely fixed, and letting y_3 equal the output of this sector and y_{13} and y_{23} be the inputs of the other two sectors used in the production of y_3, we may write

$$\frac{y_{13}}{y_3} = k_1, \qquad \frac{y_{23}}{y_3} = k_2, \tag{4}$$

where, by choice of units, we can set $k_2 = 1$.

We then obtain for the average cost of sector 3

$$AC_3 = k_1 AC_1 + k_2 AC_2 = k_1 w/ce^{rt} + AC_2. \tag{5}$$

Measured in terms of labor units, i.e., holding w constant, the first term of (5) must approach zero asymptotically. Consequently, the behavior of AC_3 over time will approach that of the stagnant sector, 2.

Thus, we obtain

Proposition 2. The behavior of the average cost of an asymptotically stagnant sector will approach, asymptotically, that of the stagnant sector from which the former obtains inputs.

What is surprising about the phenomenon we are discussing is that the sectors of the economy suffering from the asymptotic stagnation problem in its most extreme form are, in reality, those providing the most "high tech" activities--those in the vanguard of innovation and change. That this is predicted by the theory should be clear from (5) which shows that the more rapid the rate of productivity growth of the sector 1 input, i.e., the greater the value of r, the more rapidly will the intertemporal behavior of AC_3 approach that of the nonprogressive sector. The intuitive reason is clear. The falling cost of the progressive sector input accounts for the initial fall in the real unit cost of the asymptotically stagnant sector. But the very fall in the cost of that input reduces its share in the total costs of the asymptotically stagnant sector, leaving the behavior of those costs to be determined by the course of the stagnant sector input. Hence, an initial period of decline in the cost of the asymptotically stagnant sector is followed by a future of rising relative cost.

Computer usage was just cited as an example of a sector 3 activity, and the behavior of its cost provides a truly striking example of our conclusion. The heterogeneity of the products involved makes it difficult to arrive at precise figures, but it has been estimated that the hardware cost of memory and of a given amount of computation may be decreasing at a compounded annual rate somewhere between 30 and 50 percent. This, surely, is not what we expect of a stagnant sector. Yet, a second set of figures indicates the obverse side of this picture. It has been estimated that the pure labor cost of the computation process has risen from some 5 percent of a microprocessor system cost in 1973 to some 80 percent of the total in 1978 (see Kubitz 1980, 143). Thus, one should not be surprised if this activity were soon to exhibit symptoms of the cost behavior of the stagnant sector.[4]

A similar phenomenon is to be observed in broadcasting. It has been suggested that the transition from live performance to television broadcasting may represent the single largest leap in productivity in the 20th century. Using virtually the same number of person-hours (in operating the theater, the means of transportation, etc. as against the work of broadcast transmission technicians, etc.), a live performance of a drama is fortunate to have an audience of 1,500, while a television broadcast of the same performance may reach 20 million persons--a 13,333-fold increase in productivity. Yet, presumably because of the very rapid growth of productivity in the process of transmission, today technical costs are reported to constitute as little as 11 percent of the cost of broadcasting.[5] This means that even though it is an industry characterized by very "high technology," it, too, for all practical purposes, may have joined the stagnant sector.

So far, it has been assumed for simplicity that there is a fixed ratio between the input quantities sector 3 derives from the progressive and the stagnant sectors. But this premise was used only for expository convenience. Over a broad range of patterns of behavior of input proportions the same sort of problems arise for sector 3.

It is intuitively obvious (and easy to confirm analytically) that the qualitative behavior patterns we are discussing become more extreme if the magnitude of the input from the stagnant sector grows, relatively, with time. But with this input growing relatively ever more expensive, that is, of course, not what should be expected to happen.

Let us, therefore, consider a case that would seem most unfavorable to our result--that in which the progressive sector input, y_{13}, is substituted at an exponential rate for the input, y_{23}, of the stagnant sector.[6] We may describe this case with the aid of the following self-explanatory relationships between the inputs and output of sector 3:

$$y_{13}/y_3 = k_1 e^{r_1 t} \qquad y_{23}/y_3 = k_2 e^{-r_2 t} \qquad r_1 \geq 0,\ r_2 \geq 0 \tag{6}$$

Then we have

$$AC_3 = AC_1\ y_{13}/y_3 + AC_2\ y_{23}/y_3$$

or

$$AC_3/AC_1 = y_{13}/y_3 + (y_{23}/y_3)\ AC_2/AC_1$$

$$= k_1 e^{r_1 t} + k_2 e^{-r_2 t}\ e^{rt}\ c/d,$$

that is

$$AC_3/AC_1 = k_1 e^{r_1 t} + k^*\ e^{(r-r_2)t}. \tag{7}$$

This will clearly increase exponentially provided that $r_2 \leq r$, that is, provided that the sector 2 input is not reduced quite as rapidly as the productivity of the progressive sector increases.

The result is, however, surprisingly more robust than this observation suggests. While the condition $r \geq r_2$ is sufficient, it is by no means necessary for AC_3/AC_1 to grow exponentially. Indeed, so long as $r_1 > 0$, i.e., so long as a reduction in y_{23}/y_3 requires some increase in y_{13}/y_3, the result must eventually hold. For the last term in equation (7) must approach zero asymptotically if $r < r_2$, so that $AC_3/AC_1 \cong k_1 e^{r_1 t}$. The explanation, in economic terms, is that a reduction in the use of the stagnant sector's input per unit of output 3 requires some substitution of sector 1 input per unit of sector 3 output, and, with sector 1 as numeraire, this necessitates a progressive rise in the cost of the sector 1 input per unit of output of sector 3. Of course, in practice that rise need not be exponential, but it must keep going on as time passes.[7]

Thus a sector of type 3 may, perhaps, be compared to an astronomical nova whose very brightness, attributable to the rapidity with which it burns its fuel, presages its early extinction.

R&D AND SECTOR 3 ACTIVITIES

The key to the argument that follows is that the characteristics of R&D activity fall somewhere between those of a sector that is purely stagnant and one that can be described as nova-like. In effect, R&D may, itself, be taken to use, preponderantly, two types of input, which may be described as mental labor (i.e., human time) and technological equipment such as computers, which it has been argued, constitute an activity approximating the characteristics of sector 3. It is not difficult to show that if this is a valid characterization of R&D activity, then it, too, must behave very much like a sector 3 activity. Intuitively, the reason is clear. For in that case the costs of each of its two inputs must ultimately begin to behave like those of the stagnant sector.

But this conclusion also suggests others. One of the immediate implications is that, depending upon the price (and income) elasticity of the (derived) demand for R&D, it is possible that the rising relative cost of its product will lead to a reduction in its use relative to other inputs with the passage of time.

Moreover, we will show that in our model it is perfectly consistent for output of R&D to decline, for total expenditure on R&D to rise, both absolutely and as a share of GNP, and for the amount of labor time devoted to R&D relative to GNP to fall. We will see also that, if these conclusions hold, they may help to account for the curious empirical observations with which this discussion began.

ON THE BEHAVIOR OF DEMANDS AND OUTPUTS

The behavior of the demands for the products of the different sectors, that is, the responses of quantities demanded to endogenous developments in the economy described by our model, must play a key role in the analysis. For that must, in turn, determine relative outputs, expenditures, and the allocation of the labor force. Can anything be said about the likely character of those demands and its implications for the behavior of the economy? Of course, virtually any pattern of demand behavior is possible. However, a few simple premises can narrow the range of possibilities considerably.

The two crucial demand issues in our model are the response of quantity demanded to the rise in real income generated by the growing productivity of the progressive and the asymptotically stagnant sectors, and its response to changes in the relative costs (and prices) of the different sectors. Let us assume for simplicity that the effects of income and price on quantity demanded are multiplicative, i.e., that the effect of each of these two variables is represented by an expression of its own and that the demand function is the product of these two expressions. In addition, let us take the price elasticities of demand to be constant. Then, assuming the price of sector i to be proportionate to its average cost, we obtain the demand functions

$$y_i = f^i(y)AC_i^{-E_i} \qquad (i = 1, 2, 3) \tag{8}$$

where y is the economy's total real income at a given time and E_i is the price elasticity of demand for good i, which is assumed constant over time. Taking the E_i^{th} root of both sides, we obtain readily

$$\frac{y_1^{1/E_1}}{y_j^{1/E_j}} = g^j(y)\,\frac{AC_j}{AC_1} \quad (j = 2, 3). \tag{9}$$

Thus, if all E_i satisfy $0 < E_i^* \leq E_i \leq E_i^{**} < \infty$, where E_i^*, E_i^{**} are constants and since by (2) and (5) AC_j/AC_1 must ultimately increase without limit, we obtain

Proposition 3. Unless income elasticities of demand are such as to offset the price effects, so long as all price elasticities are bounded away from both zero and infinity, y_1 must ultimately increase without limit relative to the output of either the stagnant or the asymptotically stagnant sectors. That is, the relative demand for the two latter outputs must ultimately approach zero.

Great care must be taken in interpreting this proposition. First, it tells us little about what will happen before sufficient time has elapsed for the variables to approach their limiting values. Second, even if the quantities demanded from sectors 2 and 3 do fall toward zero relative to the quantity demanded from sector 1, it does not mean that either y_2 and y_3 must decline at all, in absolute terms. The point is that the increasing productivity of sector 1 and its consequent decline in cost may elicit such an expansion in quantity demanded as to swamp any rise in y_2 or y_3. Finally, in any particular pair of sectors the behavior of real income may obviously overcome the price effects encompassed in Proposition 4, as seems, at least so far, to have been true of the public's demand for health care relative to that for manufactured goods.[8]

Our conclusion about the prospective asymptotic behavior of relative outputs really makes a point that is fairly obvious. With relative prices of the products of the stagnant and asymptotically stagnant sectors rising without limit, unless income or price elasticities of demand are sharply biased in favor of these products, the relative quantities of these items demanded must ultimately fall and may very well fall toward zero. The bit of formal analysis encompassed in (8) and (9) is really no more than an algebraic restatement of this intuitive conclusion which perhaps overstates it somewhat and renders it excessively rigid.

R&D: OBSERVATIONS ON RELATIVE EXPENDITURE AND EMPLOYMENT

We turn now to the empirical observations with which our discussion began--the apparent relative rise in R&D outlays and the reported fall in R&D personnel relative to manufacturing output. We will show how in our model expenditure on the output of either the stagnant or the asymptotically stagnant sector may increase over time relative to that of the progressive sector, and yet the ratio of the labor input of either non-progressive sector may fall relative to the output of the progressive sector. This may seem like a curious comparison, but it encompasses precisely the sort of paradoxical relationship with which the paper began--the observation that expenditure on R&D was apparently rising relative to the value of manufacturing output, while the number of research scientists was reported to be falling relative to output.

Specifically, we wish to show

Proposition 4. Taking prices to be proportionate to average costs, the value of the output of the asymptotically stagnant sector relative to that of the progressive sector,

$$\frac{\text{value of } y_3}{\text{value of } y_1} = \frac{AC_3 y_3}{AC_1 y_1},$$

may be rising while the relative size of the labor force of the asymptotically stagnant sector,

$$\frac{L_3}{AC_1 y_1},$$

relative to the value of manufacturing output, is falling.

To show that there is no contradiction between these two assertions it is again only necessary to produce an example. But we will do more than this, showing that the circumstances in which both will hold simultaneously need not be considered unusual or unlikely a priori.

For our example showing that both assertions can be valid at the same time, let us assume once more that, because the date t exceeds some value, t^*, AC_2 is, thereafter, a close approximation to AC_3, in accord with (5).

By (3) we then have

$$\frac{AC_3 y_3}{AC_1 y_1} \cong \frac{ce^{rt}}{d} \frac{y_3}{y_1}. \tag{10}$$

In addition, we assume

$$L_3 \cong y_3/m \text{ , m constant.} \tag{11}$$

In that case, if, say,

$$y_3/y_1 = he^{-r_3 t} \quad 0 \le r_3 \le \tag{12}$$

it is clear by (10) that

$$\frac{AC_3}{AC_1}\frac{y_3}{y_1} \cong \frac{che^{(r-r_3)t}}{d} \quad \text{will be increasing} \tag{13}$$

while taking y_1 as numeraire, so that $p_1 = AC_1 = 1$,

$$L_3/AC_1y_1 = y_3/y_1m = he^{-r_3t}/m \quad \text{will be decreasing.} \tag{14}$$

Since our objective is merely to show that (13) and (14) are possible simultaneously, i.e., to demonstrate that they are not inconsistent, this completes our proof of Proposition 4.

Clearly, the result could have been demonstrated with the aid of a range of relationships far more general than (10) and (11) so that we are not dealing with a case that is pathological or even particularly special. This is confirmed when we consider what is going on here. In essence, the source of the behavior we are observing is the rising relative cost of the output of asymptotically stagnant sector 3 (or, rather, the falling absolute labor cost of the output of progressive sector 1). Thus, if total expenditure on y_3 increases but does not do so in proportion to the rise in its relative cost, then y_3 will fall relative to y_1, and, taking y_1 as numeraire, y_3 will then fall relative to the value of y_1. Since L_3 is proportionate to y_3 the result follows.

In short, the empirical observations on R&D expenditures and employment relative to manufacturing output are perfectly consistent with the behavior of our model. They are, in fact, to be expected whenever expenditures on R&D rise but not by an amount sufficient to make up for the rising relative cost of R&D attributable (in our model) to its property as an asymptotically stagnant sector.

ON PRODUCTIVITY AND GROWTH

So far we have assumed that in the progressive sector the productivity of labor is growing at a constant percentage rate. However, that leaves out of the system a crucial relationship--that between R&D and the technical change in sector 1 that makes for its productivity growth. Thus, instead of r being a constant, it must be a function of y_{31}, the quantity of R&D used as an input by sector 1.

We may, as an approximation, take sector 1 to be the sole consumer of the output of the R&D sector 3, so that $y_{31} = y_3$. Then, we may write for any period, t,

$$r = R(y_3)\ , \quad R' > 0\ , \quad R(0) = a \tag{15}$$

where a, the autonomous growth rate, is that attributable to independent invention and innovation that is not the product of the organized R&D sector. The remainder of the story is not quite as obvious as it may seem, though it begins in a predictable manner. Because sector 3 is asymptotically stagnant, ultimately its average cost and, hence, its relative price must begin to rise. With the exceptions noted in Proposition 3, demand for y_3 and, hence, its use by sector 1 will decline toward zero. With that, by (15), r will also fall. So far, then, the scenario is one in which the asymptotically stagnant character of the R&D activity acts as a brake on the rate of productivity growth of the economy.[9]

But the decline in r itself will lead to a deceleration in the relative price of R&D, and that, in turn, will serve to slow down the decline in demand for its product and the resulting fall in the value of r. The natural questions, then, are whether all of this is compatible with some sort of equilibrium in which r, p_3, and y_3 attain some steady state, and if so, what the character of that steady state will be.

It is easy to show that such a limiting steady state is possible. We will show this first with a vastly oversimplified model, leaving until later the introduction of the complications that necessarily arise out of the relationships that have just been described. For analytic tractability, we will assume, first, that the relationships are all linear and involve only the values of the pertinent variables in two adjacent periods--a premise that is actually a distortion of the model, as we will see later.

We then take the growth rate, r_{t+1}, in period t+1 to be a linear function of y_{3t} (which we interpret as professional R&D output in the preceding period, as distinguished from amateur invention, which corresponds to the constant a), giving us

$$r_{t+1} = a + by_{3t}, \tag{16}$$

where simultaneously, the quantity of professional R&D output demanded and, hence, made available is taken to be a declining linear function of its price, $y_{3t} = u - v\,p_{3t}$. We also adopt for simplicity the unsupported premise that r_t, the rate of productivity growth in sector 1, and real price in sector 3, AC_{3t}, are proportionate so that $p_{3t} = c^*r_t$. We may then take as our demand function for R&D

$$y_{3t} = u - c^*vr_t\ , \tag{17}$$

where c* depends upon the units of measurement and which, when combined with (16), gives us the first order linear difference equation

$$r_{t+1} = a + bu - c^*bvr_t, \tag{18}$$

which determines the time path of r_t and, together with either (16) or (17), that of y_{3t}. For convenience, we select units so that $c^* = 1$. The standard properties of difference equations indicate immediately that there will be a steady state equilibrium

$$r_e = (a + bu)/(1 + bv),$$

which r_t will approach in a stable manner, provided that $bv < 1$, that is, provided b, the marginal induced change in productivity rate, and v, the marginal response in demand for R&D to changes in r, are both sufficiently small.

That is hardly surprising. What is perhaps more unexpected is that because of the negative sign of the coefficient of r_t in (18), the time paths of r_t and y_{3t} will be oscillatory, in the classic cobweb pattern. The reason is not difficult to explain intuitively. A rise in y_{3t}, professional R&D output, speeds growth, which in turn aggravates the cost disease afflicting asymptotically stagnant sector 3 and, hence, depresses its output in the ensuing period. In the next period, the story is therefore reversed, and so the variables proceed, periods of rapid growth alternating with periods of stagnation induced through the R&D sector's behavior.

But this is, as has been hinted, a distorted tale, though its story, as we will see, is not entirely misleading. The problem resides in relationship (17), which assumes away the lasting influence of earlier R&D outputs.

Equation (17) should be a demand function with r_t replaced by $p_3 = c^*AC_3 = AC_3$. And in the model with which we are now dealing, the analogues of (3) and (5) should now yield (writing $D_t = r_0 + r_1 + \ldots + r_t$) something like

$$AC_{3t} = se^{(r_0 + r_1 + \ldots + r_t)} = se^{D_t}, \tag{19}$$

meaning that current AC is determined by past productivity growth. Let us, therefore, assume for simplicity that the demand function for R&D takes the logarithmic form

$$y_{3t} = u^* - v\ell_N P_{3t} = u^* - v\ell_N AC_{3t}.$$

We then obtain from (19)

$$y_{3t} = u^* - v\ell_N s - vD_t \equiv u - vD_t.$$

This, together with the definition of D_t in (19), gives us the following system:

$$\begin{cases} y_{3t} = u - vD_t \\ D_t = D_{t-1} + r_t \end{cases} \tag{20}$$

which, together with (16), is readily shown to constitute a system of two simultaneous difference equations

$$\begin{cases} r_{t+1} = a + bu - bvD_t \\ D_{t+1} = D_t + r_{t+1}. \end{cases} \tag{21}$$

This system has the characteristic equation

$$\begin{vmatrix} x & bv \\ -x & x-1 \end{vmatrix} = x^2 + (bv - 1)x = 0 \tag{22}$$

whose roots are clearly,

$$x_1 = 0, \quad x_2 = 1 - bv.$$

Since in equilibrium we have $D_{t+1} = D_t = D_e$, (21) immediately yields the equilibrium values

$$r_{t+1} = r_e = 0 \quad D_e = (a + bu)/bv, \tag{23}$$

and we have the general solution

$$\begin{aligned} r_t &= r_o (1 - bv)^t \\ D_t &= (a + bu)/bv + k(1 - bv)^t \end{aligned} \tag{24}$$

where k is an appropriately selected constant. This system is stable if and only if $-1 < (1 - bv) < 1$, i.e., if $0 < bv < 2$. Its behavior will be nonoscillatory if $bv < 1$, in which case r_t will decrease monotonically and asymptotically from r_0 toward its limit, zero.

In other words, in that case, the growth of the economy's productivity will decline monotonically toward its zero limit value.

This suggests that in our model the asymptotically stagnant behavior of our R&D sector may ultimately drag down the productivity growth of our economy toward a point where that growth stops entirely.

But some thought about the matter suggests that there is something wrong with this conclusion--that it goes more than a bit too far. If we insert our conclusion $r_e = 0$ into (16), we see that in equilibrium we must have

$$r_e = 0 = a + by_{3e} \quad \text{or } y_{3e} = -a/b < 0.$$

In other words, it implies that in equilibrium professional R&D output must be negative! This absurd conclusion follows from the presence of the term $\underline{a}$, representing autonomous R&D activity. If this activity is not to keep productivity, prices, and other variables changing forever, it is necessary for r_t, the rate of productivity growth, to reach zero despite the work of autonomous inventors, and only a negative R&D output can achieve this result.

It may seem that the requirement $r_e = 0$ is just a definitional artifact, following from the connotation we have given to D_t and the resulting tautological relationship $D_{t+1} = D_t + r_{t+1}$. In other words, the problem seems to arise from the requirement that in equilibrium no variable changes its value with the passage of time, whereas, with a > 0 at most we can expect a growth equilibrium, i.e., constancy of growth rate. However, there is more to the matter. A simple alternative model which captures our required relationships by being expressed in terms of the growth rates of the variables, rather than the variables themselves, will now be described, and we will see that it leads to a similar difficulty. It will also suggest the nature of the appropriate solution.

To express our relationships in terms of growth rates, this time instead of (19), we employ

$$\Delta AC_{3t+1} = \Delta P_{3t+1} = a + by_{3t}, \text{ or } y_{3t} = -a/b + \Delta P_{3t+1}/b. \qquad (25)$$

That is, we do not take current output of R&D to determine the absolute level of the next period's level of average cost = price of R&D, but only to determine the change in the values of these variables from their levels during the preceding period. Thus, implicitly, we adhere to the conclusion that the absolute value AC_{3t} depends on R&D output in all preceding periods. Next, since it is P_{3t} rather than P_{3t} that we now want as one of our structural variables, instead of the demand equation $y_{3t} = u - vP_{3t}$, we write

$$\Delta y_{3t+1} = y_{3t+1} - y_{3t} = -v \, \Delta P_{3t+1} \qquad (26)$$

Using (25) to eliminate y_3 from (26) we obtain

$$\Delta P_{3t+1}/b - \Delta P_{3t}/b = -v \, \Delta P_{3t}, \text{ or } \Delta P_{3t+1} = (1 - bv)\Delta P_{3t}. \qquad (27)$$

This equation is, clearly, expressed in terms of the growth rate of P_3, as we desired. Yet, it does not eliminate our difficulties. Its equilibrium value is $P_{3t} = 0$, i.e., it again requires zero absolute change in prices. Moreover, (25) and (26) also give us a difference equation for y_{3t} (not y_{3t}):

$$y_{3t+1} = -va + (1 - bv)y_{3t}. \qquad (28)$$

Not surprisingly, (27) and (28) again have the characteristic root x = 1 -

bv, and (28) again yields the negative equilibrium value $y_{3e} = -a/b < 0$ obtained by setting $y_{3t+1} = y_{3t} = y_{3e}$. We see that this disturbing conclusion has a disturbing degree of robustness. A bit more consideration indicates the source of the problem in the model as constructed, so long as autonomous R&D continues to be positive because $a > 0$. Then, even if professional R&D output assumes its minimal feasible value, $y_{3t} = 0$, r_t will continue to be positive and P_{3t} will continue to rise. Our linear demand equation therefore requires y_{3t} to continue to fall further below its initial zero value, and, therefore, to become negative.

Clearly, what is at fault is the linearity of the demand equation. That equation must be supplemented by a non-negativity requirement $y_{3t} \geq 0$. A phase diagram (Fig. 1) now shows us how this changes matters. In the figure, line AB is simply the graph of our difference equation (28) drawn on the assumption that its slope $1 - bv$ satisfies $0 < (1 - bv) < 1$ so that the solution time path is stable and nonoscillatory. Because of the negative intercept, $-va$, the 45° line and AB intersect at E in the negative quadrant. Thus, without the non-negativity requirement, $y_{3t} \geq 0$, the time path will be indicated by the broken line a b c d e . . ., which converges to the negative equilibrium point E. But with the addition of the non-negativity condition, the resulting nonlinear difference equation is represented by the piecewise linear graph OHB, rather than by AB, and y_{3t} will now converge to the origin.

With the resulting solution we will have $r_t = a$, and the relative cost of R&D will continue to rise. But by then, R&D will be reduced entirely to an amateur activity carried out by inventors to whom the work represents what is, in essence, a mere hobby.

ALTERNATIVE SCENARIOS

While this is a fitting tale for telling by a dismal scientist, it does not represent the only possible outcome. As is well known, depending on the value of bv, the time path of our variables may be oscillatory, and it may either be stable or unstable. This depends upon the magnitudes of $b = \partial r_t/\partial y_{3t-1}$, the marginal response in growth rate to professional R&D output, and $-v = \partial y_{3t}/\partial P_{3t}$, the marginal response of the demand for professional R&D output with respect to its price. Clearly, we expect $b > 0$ and $v > 0$. The magnitude of $bv \cong \partial r_t/\partial P_{3t-1}$ has not been directly estimated in the existing literature, though instinct would suggest that it is likely to be relatively small and certainly not considerably greater than unity.[10]

Now, it is easy to verify that the following relationships hold between the magnitude of bv and the qualitative properties of our time paths:

bv	time path
(a) $bv < 0$	unstable, nonoscillatory
(b) $0 < bv < 1$	stable, nonoscillatory
(c) $1 < bv < 2$	stable, oscillatory
(d) $bv > 2$	unstable, oscillatory

We can clearly rule out case (a) and, almost certainly, case (d). This leaves us with (b), which was discussed in the previous section, and (c), which, though it is oscillatory, has exactly the same low growth equilibri-

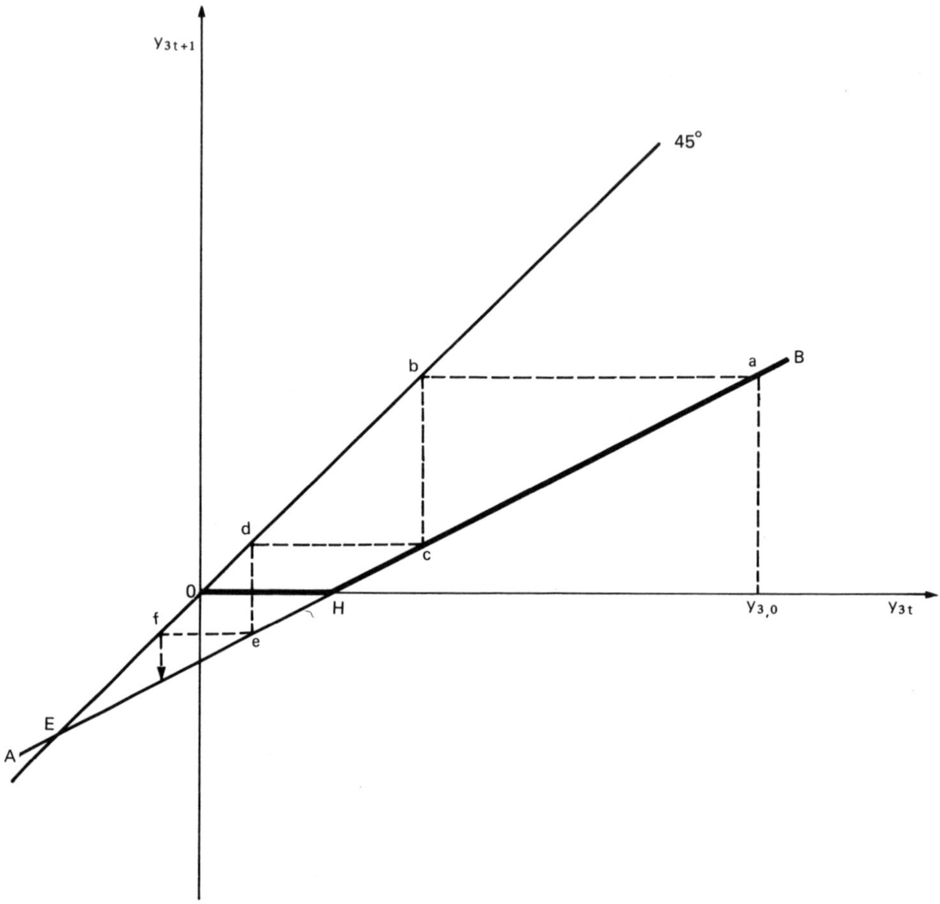

Figure 1

um solution as (b). Thus, the variety of available solutions does not seem to offer much room for improvement in the direction toward which the system moves.

AN ALTERNATIVE LINEAR MODEL

Instead of the premise that the demand function is logarithmic, we may prefer to use a linearity assumption. We do so in the following model. As before, we employ (16) as our linear relationship between R&D output and productivity growth in sector 1. In addition, we adopt the linear R&D demand function

$$y_{3t} = c - k\, P_{3t} \tag{29}$$

along with the premise that the absolute rate of change in R&D price is proportionate to the rate of growth in productivity, i.e., that

$$P_{3t+1} - P_{3t} = hr_t. \tag{30}$$

From (29) we see that $y_{3t+1} - y_{3t} = -k(P_{3t+1} - P_{3t})$, so that, substituting this into (30), we have

$$y_{3t+1} = y_{3t} - kh\, r_t. \tag{31}$$

This, together with (16), now constitutes the basic dynamic model in the variables y_t and r_t. Its characteristic equation is

$$\begin{vmatrix} x & -b \\ kh & x-1 \end{vmatrix} = x^2 - x + bkh = 0.$$

Its roots x_1, x_2 must satisfy

$$x_1 + x_2 = 1,\ x_1x_2 = bkh > 0. \tag{32}$$

It follows immediately that if the roots are real, they must both be positive because if only one of them were positive, we would have $x_1x_2 \leq 0$, and if neither were positive, then $x_1 + x_2 \leq 0$, in either case violating (32). It follows that the system must then also be stable because either $x_1 \geq 1$ or $x_2 \geq 1$ must imply $x_1 + x_2 > 1$, again violating (32).

The only remaining possibility is that x_1, x_2 are complex. Here the roots must be given by

$$1/2 \pm [(1/4) - bkh]^{1/2} = 1/2 + i(bkh - 1/4)^{1/2}$$

whose absolute value is

$$(1/4 + bkh - 1/4)^{1/2} = (bkh)^{1/2}.$$

Thus the roots will be complex if $bkh > 1/4$ and it will then be stable if $bkh < 1$.

Equilibrium in this case involves zero productivity growth by (31) because $y_{3t+1} = y_{3t}$ implies $r_t = 0$. Then, by (16) professional R&D output must again run into the negativity problem because we again appear to obtain

$$y_e = -a/b \ .$$

This can, of course, be dealt with in exactly the same manner as it was in our discussion of the preceding model.

A FIRST-ORDER NONLINEAR MODEL

Next, we construct a nonlinear model designed to cope with the fact that if we adopt a linear demand function for R&D (29), then the nonlinear relationship (19) between the growth rate in manufacturing productivity and the average cost of R&D lead unavoidably to a nonlinear dynamic model.

The point is that equation (31) in the preceding model is not precisely what is wanted, since it asserts that the absolute growth in R&D price is proportionate to r_t, the percentage growth in manufacturing productivity. Instead, one should employ a relationship such as

$$(P_{3t+1} - P_{3t})/P_{3t} = hr_{t+1}, \tag{33}$$

where by appropriate choice of units we can set h = 1. But by (29)

$$(P_{3t+1} - P_{3t})/P_{3t} = (y_{3t+1} - y_{3t})/(y_{3t} - c).$$

Combining this result with (16) and (33), we obtain the first-order nonlinear difference equation

$$a + by_{3t} = (y3t+1 - y3t)/(y3t - c) \quad \text{or} \tag{34}$$

$$y_{3t+1} = -ca + (1 + a - cb)y_{3t} + by_{3t}^2. \tag{35}$$

Graphically, (34) has a phase diagram represented by curve AB in Figure 2.

The equilibrium requirement y3t+1 = y3t = y3 immediately yields the quadratic equation

$$by_3^2 + (a - cb)y_3 - ca = 0 \tag{36}$$

whose roots are readily shown to be $y_3 = c$ and $y_3 = -a/b$, as depicted in the graph. However, the first of these is not a stable equilibrium, as is readily confirmed from the derivative of (34) $dy_{3t+1}/dy_{3t} = -cb + a + 1 + 2by_{3t} = cb + a + 1 > 1$ at $y_{3t} = u$.

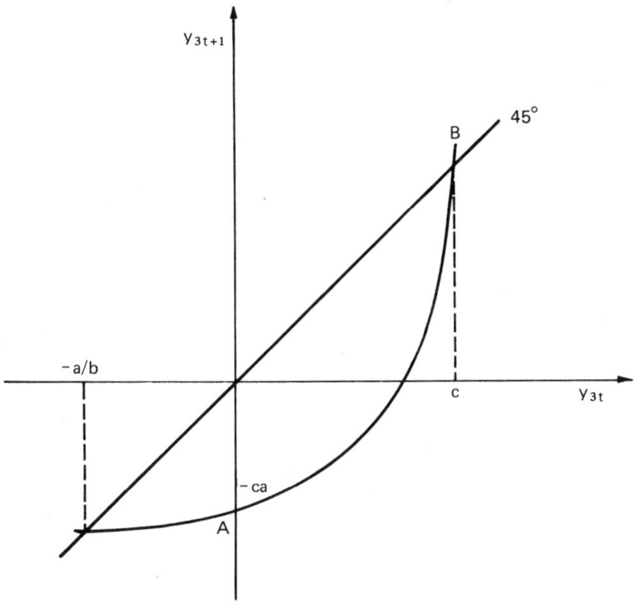

Figure 2

A SECOND-ORDER NONLINEAR MODEL

Finally, suppose on the RHS of (33) hr_t were to appear instead of hr_{t+1}. Then (34) becomes

$$a + by_{3t-1} = (y_{3t+1} - y_{3t})/(y_{3t} - c),$$

which can be rewritten as

$$y_{3t} = -ca + (1 - a)y_{3t-1} - cy_{3t-2} + by_{3t}y_{3t-2}. \tag{37}$$

This is a second-order nonlinear difference equation whose equilibrium values, for which $y_t = y_{t-1} = y_{t-2} = y_e$, are easily seen to yield (36), whose solutions, as before, are $y_e = -a/b$ and $y_e = c$.

On dealing with second-order nonlinear difference equations, it is not inherently difficult to find the candidate equilibrium points. One just substitutes $y_t = ye$, $\forall_t$ into the equation and solves for the value(s) of y_e. Stability of any such equilibrium point, y_e, can be investigated by linear approximation.

Let the equation be

$$y_t = f(y_{t-1}, y_{t-2}, \ldots, y_{t-h}) \tag{38}$$

Then calculate its partial derivatives $f_1(\cdot)$, $f_2(\cdot)$, . . . and substitute y_e for the various y's in these derivatives. Let the resulting values be designated by $f_1(y_e)$, $f_2(y_e)$, ... Next, form the approximating linear difference equation

$$y_t = f_1(y_e)y_{t-1} + f_2(y_e)y_{t-2} + \ldots + f_h(y_e)y_{t-h} \tag{39}$$

Then the stability of y_e as an equilibrium point for (39) would presumably tell us about its local stability for (38). An existence and uniqueness proof for (1) is trivial. Simply select any set of initial values y^0_{t-1}, . . ., y^0_{t-h} and substitute them into (38), yielding y^0_t. Next, define $y^1_{t-1} = y^0_t$, . . ., $y^1_{t-h} = y^0_{t-h+1}$, and substitute these values into (38) to yield y^1_t, and repeat the process. This procedure obviously gives us a time path for y given the initial values of the variables. It will also be unique if $f(\cdot)$ is a single valued function of its arguments.

CONCLUDING COMMENTS

The prime analytic contribution of our model consists in its recognition that outlays on R&D and rate of growth of productivity can and must be considered to be determined endogenously and simultaneously. Obviously, we expect an increase in R&D expenditure to stimulate productivity growth, albeit with some lag. However, the very rate of productivity growth in other sectors contributed by R&D affects the relative cost of R&D and, arguably, tends to increase that relative cost. Thus, the very success of the work of the R&D sector may sow the seeds of a future price impediment to demand for its output. While the resulting time path may not be smooth, but may, rather, prove to be characterized by oscillations, the general direction of the mechanism is clear. Inherently, it is a mechanism which, taken by itself, may tend to push the economy in the direction of stagnation. That conclusion is not meant to imply the absence of other forces working in the opposite direction or in directions that are altogether more difficult to predict. However, the analysis does call our attention to one set of endogenous relationships that may help to explain a portion of the productivity problem and may help to account for its intractability.

In any event, the model is intended to serve as a contribution to the formal analysis of the mechanism of productivity growth. Admittedly, it works in an oversimple manner, omitting all sorts of considerations that are undoubtedly of considerable importance in reality. Yet at this stage it is probably too much to expect a workable model that deals with anything approaching the full range of issues and complexities. Rather, we are, at least for the moment, content to have been able to offer a model that works at all.

NOTES

The authors are grateful to the Division of Information Science and Technology of the National Science foundation for its support of the research reported here.

1 See National Science Foundation, National Patterns of R&D Resources, Publication NSF 78-313, 1978, Washington, D.C., Government Printing Office. This figure refers to the decline in the total "full-time equivalent number of R&D scientists and engineers" employed in manufacturing and does not distinguish between those employed in military or space-related R&D. An industry breakdown is also provided by SIC code, which unfortunately does not by itself enable one to break out military or space-related R&D. However, there is one industry that does seem to fit predominantly in this category, the aircraft and missile industry. If we exclude the R&D scientists and engineers employed in this industry, the total figure shows a slight increase between 1970 and 1975 of 0.5 percent. On the other hand, manufacturing output in constant dollars rose by 9.3 percent during this period (Economic Report of the President, 1981, p. 278). Therefore, scientists and engineers employed in nonmilitary or non-space-related R&D showed, at least, a relative decline to manufacturing output.

2 The figures reported here, taken literally, are somewhat misleading. The bulk of the net increase of the labor force employed in the services has come from agriculture, and the share of service employment in the nonfarm, nonresidential business sector has remained almost constant over the postwar period. But for at least some services it is not possible to measure output directly (teaching and many government services are noteworthy examples). Consequently, it is customary to measure the quantities of such outputs in terms of the inputs used up in supplying them. Since the supply of most such services is quite labor-intensive, it is not surprising that the statistics on their share of employment and their share of output should behave similarly. However, we will see that there are analytical reasons for suspecting that the reality of the matter is rather more complicated.

3 It makes no difference to the analysis whether sector 3's second input is y_2 or is labor itself, since both costs behave similarly. That is, $AC_2 = w/b$, by(2), and the average cost of labor to industry is simply w. Indeed, we can encompass the supply of y_2 and labor to industry 3 in a single imaginary portmanteau sector which offers them both and which is clearly stagnant. If sector 3 uses L_3 hours of labor and y_{23} units of y_2 per unit of y_3 produced, then writing $y_{23} = aL_{23}$ it is clear that a unit of output 3 requires $L_3 + L_{23}$ hours of labor altogether. Thus, we may invent a fictitious output y_2^* satisfying $y_2^*/a = L_3 + L_{23}$ as the product of the portmanteau stagnant sector which supplies both labor and y_2 to sector 3.

Matters grow more complex in an input-output world in which the progressive and stagnant sectors use one another's products as inputs, but the qualitative behavior of the model is, essentially, unaffected. This is shown in Baumol and Wolff (1980).

4 Of course, such developments can be expected to give rise to attempts to offset them to whatever extent is permitted by the cost and benefits of the offsetting measures. In the case of computing, effort has been devoted to the design of equipment that reduces the need for the expenditure of time on the creation and modification of software. Some observers have even expressed hope that this can lead to a progressive reduction in the share of wages and salaries in the cost of computation. However, if hardware costs continue to fall at their current rate, it is hard to believe that the proportion of cost devoted to wages and salaries can decline for any protracted period.

5 "Television Financial Data 1980, FCC Financial Figures," Broadcasting, Vol. 101, August 10, 1981, p. 51.

6 We would expect some substitution like this, since the relative price of the input from the stagnant sectors is rising.

7 This is easily proved by substitution of a more general relationship for (6) with $d(y_{13}/y_3)/dt > 0$ and $d(y_{23}/y_3)dt < 0$. It is then trivial to prove that if $\lim y_{23}/y_3 > 0$ (as must be true by the definition of the asymptotically stagnant sector), then AC_3/AC_1 must ultimately rise.

8 Here we must exercise extreme caution in our casual empiricism. The share of GNP devoted to health care, i.e., the relative expenditure on this service, has undoubtedly been rising. But at least part of this is accounted for by the very great rise of relative prices in that sector. It follows that the real quantity purchased, if it could somehow be measured, may actually have fallen relatively to the output of other sectors. Perhaps a better example is the growing share of the population that has been demanding a college degree despite its rising relative price. Since college enrollment is largely concentrated among individuals in the 18 to 22 age bracket, the appropriate measure of average demand is the percentage of individuals in this age bracket who are enrolled as undergraduates. Between 1950 and 1975, this fraction increased from 0.236 to 0.418 or by a factor of 1.77. (Source: U.S. Bureau of the Census, Current Population Reports, Series P-25; and U.S. Bureau of the Census, Statistical Abstract of the United States.) In comparison, real manufacturing output in the United States increased by a factor of 2.58 over the same period. (Source: Economic Report of the President, 1981, p. 278.) On the other hand, mean undergraduate tuition in current dollars increased by a factor of 2.79 between 1950 and 1975 (Source: Hearings Before the Special Subcommittee on Education and Labor, House of Representatives, 93rd Congress, 2nd Session, part 7, p. 62; and Statistical Abstract of the United States), while the consumer price index for manufacturing output rose by a factor of 1.83 (Source: Economic Report of the President, 1981, p. 292). Therefore, the average expenditure by the relevant age group on a college education increased relatively to expenditure on manufacturing output, though in real terms the opposite was the case.

9 Depending partly upon the expression used to measure the economy's overall rate of productivity growth, there is another influence in our model that may well work to pull this figure down. It is not difficult to show that if the share of the economy's expenditure on the output of the progressive sector declines with the passage of time, i.e., if the relative value of this sector's output decreases, its

ability to contribute to the overall productivity growth of the economy can be expected to fall even if the value of r does not decline, i.e., even if the sector's own rate of productivity growth remains steady.

10 Some estimates of related parameters are provided in the empirical literature on R&D, which may shed some light on the value of bv. These estimates have to be interpreted cautiously since they apply to different years and sectors of the economy. Moreover, the related estimates are in terms of elasticities, so that some algebraic manipulation is first required. The term bv can be written as

$$bv \cong \frac{\partial r_t}{\partial y_{3t-1}} \left(- \frac{\partial y_{3t-1}}{\partial P_{3t-1}} \right)$$

$$bv \cong \frac{\partial r}{\partial y_3/y_3} \quad \frac{1}{P_3} \quad E$$

where we are now assuming all variables are contemporaneous and dropping the time subscript for convenience and where $E = -(\partial y_3/y_3)/(\partial p_3/p_3)$ is the absolute value of the price elasticity of demand for R&D. Since estimates of the "rate of return" to R&D are available, we further transform bv to:

$$bv \cong \pi \cdot \frac{\partial(y_3/y_1)}{\partial y_3/y_3} \cdot \frac{1}{P_3} \quad E$$

where $\pi = \partial r/\partial(y_3/y_1)$ is the normally estimated rate of return to R&D (see Terleckyj 1974, for example). With further manipulation, we obtain

$$bv \cong \pi \cdot E \cdot \left(\frac{y_3/p_3}{y_1} \right) \left(1 - \frac{\partial y_1/y_1}{\partial y_3/y_3} \right).$$

Estimates of π normally run between 25 and 30 percent (see Nadiri in National Science Foundation 1977). Estimates of E are scarce, but one is provided in Nadiri and Shankerman (1981) for the Bell System of 0.3. The term $y_3/(P_3y_1)$ is the inverse of the normalization factor which we called c* in equation (17) and assumed equal to unity in the base period. It can be ignored here, or, equivalently, we can look at the value of c*bv. Finally, the term $(\partial y_1/y_1)/(\partial y_3/y_3)$ is the output elasticity of R&D. Estimates of this are usually in the order of 10 percent (see Nadiri and Wolff 1979, for example). Thus, the resulting value of bv is very likely considerably less than unity.

COMMUNICATION AND INFORMATION ECONOMICS:
New Perspectives
M. Jussawalla and H. Ebenfield (Editors)

PRODUCTIVITY AND GROWTH OF THE INFORMATION ECONOMY

Charles Jonscher

INTRODUCTION

Fritz Machlup published in 1962 a study of the extent of labor and non-labor resources used in the United States for the creation and processing of information as opposed to physical goods. Since then numerous analyses of a similar kind have been carried out; examples are those of Peter Drucker (1968), Daniel Bell (1973), Marc Porat (1977), and again Machlup (1980). Whereas the exact findings obtained depend on how information products or services are defined, the general conclusion emerging is that about half of all economic activity in the United States can be attributed to the processing of knowledge or facts rather than of physical goods and that the proportion is increasing. Studies in the United Kingdom (Wall 1977), Australia (Barnes and Lamberton 1976), and several countries in continental Europe (Organization for Economic Cooperation and Development 1981) confirm a consistent pattern of growth in this information-handling sector of the economy.

This shift of resources from the traditional productive activities of industrial and agricultural workers to primarily office-based information-handling functions constitutes one of the most striking structural changes to have taken place in the economy over the course of this century. In this chapter we are concerned especially with the implications of this shift for economic productivity. The business community is well aware of the need to distinguish between information handling (essentially white collar) and other occupational activities when analyzing industrial efficiency. A steadily increasing proportion of business costs is accounted for by office, marketing, and other information-related tasks; the fraction has reached over 30 percent in a typical manufacturing enterprise, and is higher still in the service sector. Since historically the rate of productivity growth in white-collar functions has been much lower than in shop floor production work, this trend is placing an increasingly severe constraint on overall efficiency improvement. Efforts to cut unit costs should therefore take more account of the opportunities for productivity gains in information-handling functions. This line of reasoning has been stated, for instance, by Tyler (1981).

Professional economists have not, in the main, interpreted productivity trends in this way. To identify the class of information-handling activities in the economy as a separate category or sector is unconventional. However, there are several reasons why it is useful. First among these is the fact that it is surprisingly homogeneous, for a sector of its size, in terms of certain structural characteristics and technological trends. After working extensively with data on information-related expenditures and activities, one cannot but notice the high degree of statistical regularity in the pattern of resource use. The structure of office environments, it appears, is much less varied than that of blue-collar or production activities. The number of telephones per office worker, of secretaries per manager, of computing machines per accounts clerk--indeed practically any measure of the pattern of expenditure on information resources--appear to be very stable across industries, even though the production activities of the corresponding firms and industries are extremely diverse. Thus we have in the information sector a group of activities that accounts in the United States for about one-half of all labor effort and that almost certainly displays more homogeneity than any group of remotely comparable size. This increases the validity of studying the sector on the basis of aggregate data. Furthermore, the observed regularity in the structure of information activities suggests that it may be possible to obtain models of such activities that fit a very wide range of business environments; this motivates the development of the models described in the next section.

If the relationship between information-sector growth and productivity change is to be subject to formal analysis, two prerequisites must be fulfilled.

(1) Theoretical models of the relationship between information activity and the productivity of the economy must be developed.

(2) Such models must be applied empirically, based on data on levels of resource allocation to the information sector and its counterpart, the non-information or production sector.

This chapter contains a brief overview of recent research findings, and possible future research directions, in each of these two areas.

THEORY OF THE INFORMATION-PRODUCTIVITY RELATIONSHIP

The analysis of the role of information in the economy begins with the observation that economic activity is characterized by uncertainties. The uncertainties are reduced or resolved by the acquisition, processing, and communication of information. Economists have in recent years developed many models in which information is used to effect a reduction in some type of economic uncertainty. An early contribution to the literature on the economics of information is a paper of that title by Stigler (1961). Stigler considered the searching behavior of agents who were imperfectly informed as to the price of a commodity and could, at some cost, sample prices from a random distribution. The theory of price search has since been taken up by many other authors. Models of the reactions of agents to price distributions have been supplemented by theories that attempt to explain the existence of price dispersion; a number of these theories were presented at a symposium on the economics of information held at Stanford University in 1975. Other researchers have been concerned with the analysis of information not about prices but about some other attribute of a product or service offered for sale. The first formal analysis of market behavior in the presence of uncertainty about product quality was published by Akerlof (1970). The papers presented at the 1973 Princeton University conference on the economics of information were concerned principally with the mechanisms of signaling and screening which arise in competitive markets in the presence of uncertainty about some product attribute. Akerlof (1976) considered information transfer through a costly signal; Salop and

Salop (1976) discussed self-selection devices in the labor market, in which applicants are induced through the pricing scheme to reveal true information about themselves by their market behavior; Rothschild and Stiglitz (1976) analyzed an insurance market, where the product attribute about which there is imperfect information is each individual's risk class. Numerous other approaches to the analysis of informational processes in the economy can be listed. The study of so-called signaling equilibria--the equilibria of those markets in which agents engage in some costly activity so as to signal the otherwise unobservable attributes of a product they are trading--has become an established branch of the economics of information since it was introduced by Spence (1974).

The theories referred to above are in the main concerned with the analysis of information about some quite specific parameter of interest to an agent--a parameter such as the price of a product, the productivity of a worker, or the riskiness of an insurance contract. While these models do much to improve our understanding of the effect of uncertainty in certain well-defined market situations, their applicability is not sufficiently general for our purposes. Of the 50 percent or so of the labor effect in the United States' economy that is attributable to information-handling functions, only a very small proportion can be attributed to price searching, establishing the quality of potential employees, or estimating the risk associated with a financial contract.

Models developed by the author (Jonscher 1980, 1982) attempt to provide a simple but more general theoretical framework. Specifically they consider a series of production and trading activities and establish a function

$$\eta = h(z) \tag{1}$$

linking the efficiency of the activity (η) and the level of information processing associated with it (z). The meaning of the term efficiency is defined for each application under study. The models are based on the behavior of an agent who is engaged in a single well-defined activity, such as controlling a process, monitoring a worker, searching for a price, or promoting a product. Equilibrium levels of information resource use can then be deduced by applying an optimization model (see equation (11) below).

Four examples of models yielding such a function are given in Jonscher (1982). One is a process control model in which an event arises randomly (e.g., distributed in time as a Poisson variable) which has the effect of reducing output from its normal value Y* to some lower value Y*. The long-run average frequency of occurrence is μ. The measure of information processing in this model, z, determines the average frequency with which the process is monitored and corrective action taken, in accordance with the linear relationship $\upsilon = cz$, where c is a constant. The relevant measure of efficiency, η, is the average actual output as a proportion of the ideal output Y*. We can show that under appropriately defined conditions the efficiency is approximately given by:

$$\eta = 1 - (1-\varepsilon)\mu/2cz \tag{2}$$

Thus if we define $\beta = (1-\varepsilon)\mu/2c$, we can write h(z):

$$h(z) = 1 - \beta/z \tag{3}$$

This model is valid in a wide variety of circumstances. No particular statistical distribution of either event occurrence or monitoring schedule need be specified, provided at least one is random.

Another example of such a micro-theory model is that of market signaling. A seller offers a product with some attribute q_k; the value to the buyer, V, is a function of the difference between the actual attribute q_k and the buyer's "ideal" or desired attribute q_k^*:

$$V = V_o (1 - a(q_k - q_k^*)^2) \tag{4}$$

where V_o and a are constants. We wish to determine the expected value E(V) of the transaction to the buyer as a function of the amount of information, z, which the seller provides on this attribute. The information takes the form of a signal s_k, which is distributed normally about q_k with a variance σ^2 given by:

$$\sigma^2 = \sigma_o^2 /z . \tag{5}$$

We can show that the expected value of the product to the buyer, E(V), given a quantity z of information, is:

$$E(V) = V_o (1 - 2a\sigma_o^2 /z - a(q_k - q_k^*)^2) . \tag{6}$$

We interpret the efficiency of the transaction, in expression (1), as the ratio of actual sale value E(V) to the value V_k^* when the information regarding q_k is perfect (i.e., $z = \infty$). Then, providing $a(q_k - q_k^*) << 1$,

$$h(z) = \eta = E(V)/V_k^* \approx 1 - \beta/z \tag{7}$$

where β is the constant $2a\sigma_o^2$.

These and other models described in Jonscher (1980, 1982) show that the relationship linking efficiency η and the measure of informational input or processing z frequently takes the form $\eta = 1-\beta/z$, or a close approximation to it. In each case, η is a constant which depends on the technical and informational characteristics of the activity under study. The function h(z) can actually be made consistent with a wider range of models by allowing the exponent on z to vary, yielding the form:

$$\eta = 1 - \beta z^{-\rho} . \tag{8}$$

(3) and (7) are special cases of (8) with ρ equal to unity.

Results such as (8) can be used, in conjunction with a model of optimum information input, to guide the specification of functions suitable for empirical work. The form (8) is not itself convenient for econometric applications. The expression for the equilibrium level of information input z^* which results when agents maximize private return to information activity turns out to be cumbersome; it is one of the solutions of a quadratic equation in z^*. Bearing in mind that the purpose of developing these micro-theory models is to guide the specification of suitable aggregate functions rather than to represent exactly the interaction of information and production activities, we introduce an alternative form for (1) as follows:

$$\eta = \exp(-\beta z^{-\rho}) . \tag{9}$$

We note that (8) and (9) are closely related; the former corresponds to the first two terms of the power series expansion of the exponential expression:

$$\exp(-\beta z^{-\rho}) = 1 - \beta z^{-\rho} + \frac{1}{2!}(\beta z^{-\rho})^2 - \ldots \tag{10}$$

Furthermore, the approximation is closest for values of z sufficiently large that $\beta z^{-\rho} << 1$; the empirical work reported later shows that this condition is satisfied in practice.

We can show that the use of (9) results in a more readily estimable functional relationship for the equilibrium quantity z^* of information resource input selected by agents who maximize the value of a process of transaction net of information costs. The solution of:

$$\max_z (c_P Y - c_I z) , \tag{11}$$

where c_P and c_I are unit costs of products and information inputs respectively, can be shown to be:

$$z^* = \left(\frac{c_P}{c_I}\beta\rho Y\right)^{1/(\rho+1)} . \tag{12}$$

EMPIRICAL ANALYSIS

We show in Jonscher (1982) that under certain (relatively weak) assumptions the necessary aggregation conditions are met to permit the definition of macro models which are consistent with the summation of some large but unspecified number of activities modeled as above at the micro level. A simple instance of such a macro model yields the following equilibrium ratios of information-handling labor to production labor (I/P) as a function of gross output per production worker (Y/P):

$$I/P = (\lambda\rho\beta)^{1/(\rho+1)} (Y/P)^{1/(\rho+1)} \tag{13}$$

where $\lambda\rho$ is a constant related to the share of labor in total national income. The quantities ρ and $(\lambda\rho\beta)$ in (13) can be estimated on the basis of empirical data.

We report below some interim results from the application of the model to time-series data on the United States and selected other countries. The work completed at the time of writing does not include any formal stochastic modeling. The equilibrium relationship among I, P, and Y is, in fact, readily amenable to stochastic estimation, and further statistical work along these lines is planned. However, it is not necessary to apply formal estimation procedures to observe the broad predictions of the model and compare them with actual trends, particularly if the restriction $\rho = 1$ is imposed. This restriction is implied by the selection of micro models described in the preceding section.

The task of identifying empirically the pattern of expenditures on information activities is made practicable by the very high degree of occupational specialization present in modern societies. We use occupational categories as the primary instrument for distinguishing information processing from production activity. If a person is classified in the labor statistics as a billing clerk we may be reasonably confident that his or her primary functions are to prepare and process bills; these are information-handling activities associated with the management, organization, and coordination of economic activity. Consequently, a billing clerk is classified as an information rather than production worker. Conversely, if a person is classified as a sheet metal worker we shall assume that his primary function is to work sheet metal and not to process economic information; we categorize him as a producer rather than an information processor. Sometimes the billing clerk may help to unload a delivery truck (production, not information handling), and the sheet metal worker may fill out timesheets (information handling, not production); but these activities are the exceptions rather than the rule.

A few worker types are more difficult to classify; in these cases we have to make a (sometimes rather arbitrary) choice. Actors and other entertainers, for example, do not fit the classification scheme neatly. An important instance of an ambiguous occupation is that of a foreman. While some of a typical foreman's time is spent doing the same job as his subordinates, much of it is spent monitoring, supervising, and keeping time and other records. In the analysis that follows, we allocate 50 percent of a foreman's time to information, 50 percent to production. This allocation is obviously only an approximation of the true divisions of time and effort. Fortunately for our purposes, the number of occupations for which classification problems of this kind arise is a very small proportion of the total. The great majority, perhaps 95 percent, of the working population can be identified with reasonable confidence as fitting one or the other of our categories.

Figure 1 illustrates the results of a very simple application of the model to time series data for the United States, covering the years 1900-1979. The productivity of information workers is assumed to be fixed through time. The solid line shows the actual ratio of information to total workers in the economy. The broken line shows the ratio that is predicted by the model if it is calibrated (i.e., β set so the I/P is correct) at the year 1900 and then driven by the actual rate of growth of output per production worker in subsequent decades. The result is based on a very crude interpretation of the model variables, but it is shown here because it illustrates that the broad pattern of growth information requirements predicted as a response to increasing economic output is consistent with the observed growth of resources devoted to the information sector. The fit is not perfect, especially in the early years, but the relationships implied by the model appear to be surprisingly consistent given the very long timespan over which the explanatory power of the theory is being tested.

IMPLICATIONS FOR FUTURE RESEARCH

The preliminary results of this research suggest that there is an intricate linkage between the information-handling activities and the productivity of the economy. First, growth in industrial output and efficiency results in a greater requirement for information-processing resources. Then, the information-handling sector itself becomes sufficiently large that its own internal productivity has a major effect on the overall output per worker of the economy.

If these trends are present, development of models along the lines discussed will contribute greatly to our understanding of the different rates of productivity growth in the information and production sectors. A purpose of studying differential productivity change is to improve our knowledge of the effects of information technology on overall economic growth. Information-handling activities are very different in character from production activities; they require a different mix of labor, capital, and other input resources. The information sector is not affected by the same kinds of technological advances and, as we will show, it has historically experienced a very different pattern of productivity growth than the production sector. Because of the homogeneity of information-handling activities which we noted earlier, the distinction between information and production functions might usefully supplement the conventional division of economic activity along industry lines in the study of technological change. Thus, in addition to studying productivity change by industry groups as they are conventionally defined--manufacturing, construction, utilities, and so forth--we can extract the information-handling elements of the different industries and study them separately from their production counterparts. Technological trends may be more consistent and more easily understood within the class of information activities, across industries, than within an industry, across the information/production divide. If the distinction between the information and production components of overall growth is ignored, biases may be introduced into the analysis of the determinants of productivity growth--particularly if, as we have shown, the overall balance between the two components is changing systematically through time.

A research program designed to address these problems would develop, and fit empirically, a variety of models in which information resources (labor and non-labor) are defined as distinct inputs to economic processes. Such

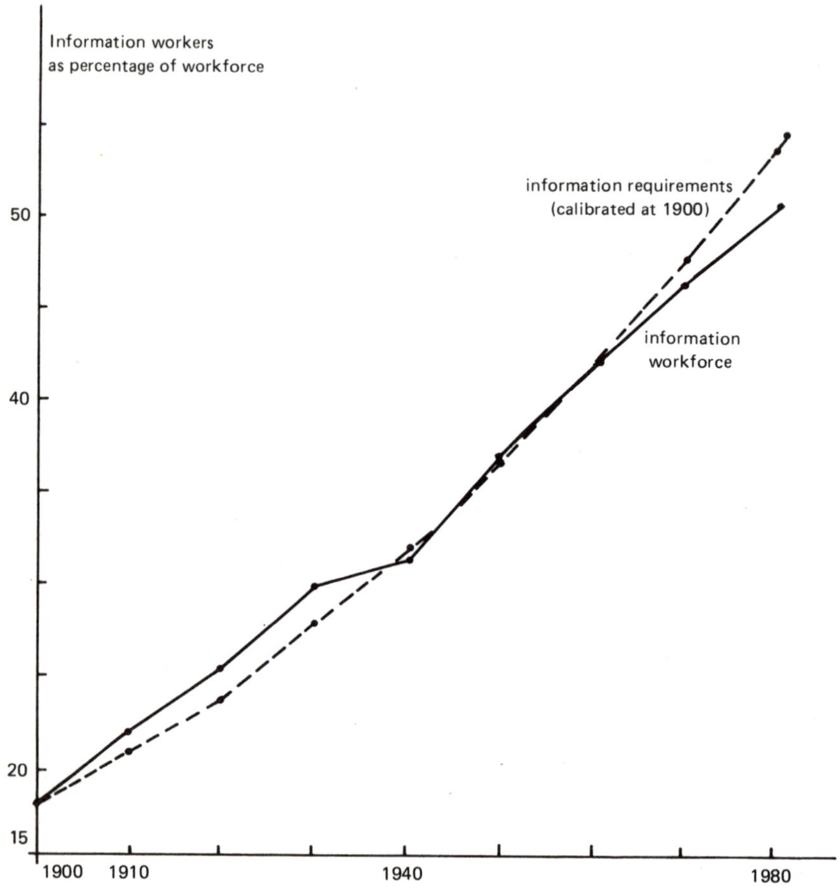

Source: Jonscher (1982).

Fig. 1. Predicted growth of information processing requirements and actual growth of U.S. information labor force, 1900–1979

models would help to: (1) improve our knowledge of the economic factors that have led to the observed growth of information resource use over the past several decades; (2) identify the degree of substitutability between information resources and other inputs to industrial activity; and (3) identify inter-industry and international differences in information requirements and substitution coefficients.

REFERENCES

1 Akerlof, G., The market for lemons: qualitative uncertainty and the market mechanism, Quarterly Journal of Economics 89 (August 1970) 488-500.

2 Akerlof, G., The economics of caste and the rat race and other woeful tales, Quarterly Journal of Economics 90 (1976) 599-618.

3 Drucker, P., The Age of Discontinuity (Harper and Row, New York, 1968).

4 Jonscher, C., Models of Economic Organizations, Ph.D. Dissertation, Dept. of Economics, Harvard Univ. (1980).

5 Jonscher, C., Productivity Change and the Growth of Information Processing Requirements in the Economy: Theory and Empirical Analysis, Dept. of Economics, Harvard Univ. (1982).

6 Machlup, F., The Production and Distribution of Knowledge in the United States (Princeton University Press, Princeton, N.J., 1962).

7 Porat, M., The Information Economy: Definition and Measurement, OT special publication 77-12(1), (U.S. Department of Commerce, 1977).

8 Rothschild, M. and Stiglitz, J., Equilibrium in competitive insurance markets: an essay on the economics of imperfect information, Quarterly Journal of Economics 90 (1976) 629-650.

9 Spence, A.M., Market Signaling: Informational Transfer in Hiring and Related Processes (Harvard University Press, Cambridge, Mass., 1974).

10 Stigler, G.J., The economics of information, Journal of Political Economy 69 (June 1961) 213-225.

11 Tyler, M., Telecommunications and productivity: the need and the opportunity, in: Moss, M.L. (ed.), Telecommunications and Productivity (Addison-Wesley Publishing Co., Reading, Mass., 1981).

COMMUNICATION AND INFORMATION ECONOMICS:
New Perspectives
M. Jussawalla and H. Ebenfield (Editors)

SCOPE AND SCALE AUGMENTING TECHNOLOGICAL CHANGE: AN APPLICATION IN THE INFORMATION SECTOR

Lawrence B. Pulley and Yale M. Braunstein

INTRODUCTION

Technological change or productivity growth is generally defined as a shift in the efficient production surface. However, the difficulties of modeling or empirically evaluating technological change have not been fully resolved. Recent efforts (Caves, Christensen, and Swanson 1981; Stevenson 1980) have sought to distinguish between shifts in the production function and movements along it by including a time or shift variable (with appropriate interaction terms) explicitly into a standard cost function specification. However, this approach can fail when technological change is predominantly scale augmenting. Furthermore, popular multiplicative (or log-additive) flexible cost functions such as the translog are not particularly well-suited for investigating properties of the technologies of multiproduct firms such as economies of scope and subadditivity, a necessary and sufficient condition for multiproduct natural monopoly (Baumol, Panzar, and Willig 1982). Multiplicative functions, for example, do not allow zero output values, making it impractical to measure the cost advantages of adding product lines (economies of scope).

Our objective in this paper is to develop a methodology to overcome some of these difficulties. We suggest a cost function specification that can be used to examine important characteristics of the production structure of multiproduct firms. We then report on a preliminary application of the approach to a firm in the information sector.

SCALE AUGMENTING TECHNOLOGICAL CHANGE

Currently popular techniques for evaluating the effects of technological change can be inappropriate for certain classes of such change. Caves, Christensen, and Swanson and Stevenson attempt to isolate shifts in from movements along the production structure by incorporating a shift variable directly into a general translog cost function approximation. Productivity growth, defined as the common rate at which all inputs can be reduced over time with outputs held fixed, is then given by $-\partial \ln C/\partial t$ where C is the dual cost function and t is the shift variable. (Operationally, the derivative is generally evaluated using the mean values of the variables.) This approach is appropriate if the effect of technological change is as depicted in Fig. 1. We consider the simple case of a single-output firm with linear cost curves and fixed input prices. The initial cost function is TC_0. Due to technological progress the cost function shifts to TC_1 in period 1. Output Y_0 is produced on TC_0 in period 0, and output Y_1 is produced when TC_1 prevails in period 1. Evaluating productivity growth as the negative of the partial derivative of the cost function with respect to the

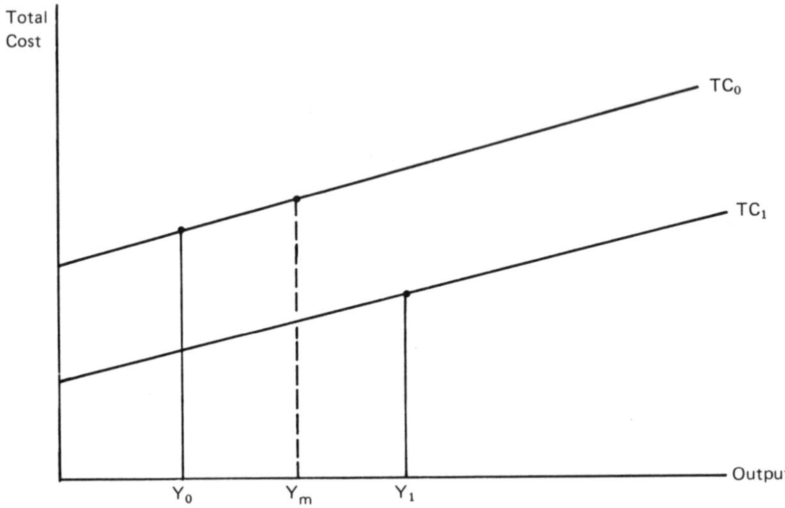

Figure 1

shift variable (evaluated at mean output Y_m) will accurately reflect the effects of technological change in this case.

Suppose, however, that technological change results in increased cost efficiencies biased in favor of larger output levels, i.e., the firm gains scale advantages. In this case the methodology described above can easily lead to nonsensical results. As an example, consider the cost functions in Fig. 2. Initial output is Y_0 on cost function TC_0. The firm changes its production technology and gains scale efficiencies, i.e., the cost function shifts to TC_1 and the firm ends up producing Y_1, exploiting some of the cost reductions at higher output levels. Suppose we attempt to estimate this cost function with a shift variable to reflect the effects of technical change. If we then evaluate productivity growth as the negative of the partial derivative of the cost function evaluated at mean output Y_m, we are led to the incorrect conclusion that technological change has produced negative productivity growth and increased costs.

In both the Caves, Christensen, and Swanson study of U.S. railroads and the Stevenson study of electric utilities there is an indication that technological progress is of the type depicted in Fig. 1 above. The shifts in the production structure appear to leave returns to scale approximately the same as before the technological change (railroads) or to actually decrease them (utilities). However, for many firms, particularly those in the information sector, technological advances need not, indeed probably will not, be scope and scale neutral. Estimating technological change for such functions using shift variables may not be warranted. In the next section we suggest a procedure for avoiding these difficulties.

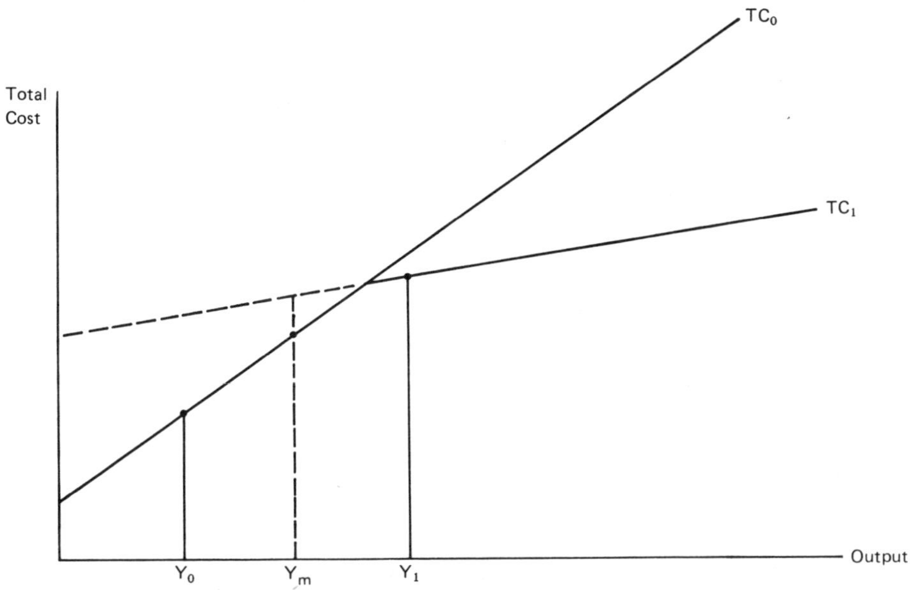

Figure 2

METHODOLOGY

The recent history of the firm under analysis in this study is probably not unlike that experienced by many firms in the information sector. During the period under analysis, the firm, which publishes indices containing abstracts of articles in technical journals, automated its data processing and retrieval capabilities. Since a major component of the firm's production activity involves data processing, the changes undertaken are potentially significant ones. The effects of this form of technological change, however, are not obvious.

Such a shift to automated data processing could lead to reduced costs for current output levels (i.e., change of the type depicted in Fig. 1) or enhanced scale opportunities for future expansion (i.e., change as in Fig. 2), or both. During our preliminary discussions, the firm's manager justified the move to automation in terms of enhanced production potential for future expansion as well as quality improvement.[1] They anticipated cost savings to be realized only as they continued to expand output. Thus, we might expect the effects of technological change to be of the sort depicted in Fig. 2 above. In the next section we will use the methodology described below to examine whether automation has increased the opportunities for expansion in terms of both the scope and scale of operations.

The dual cost function possesses certain advantages for analyzing the effects of technological change on the scale and scope characteristics of multiproduct firms. The general form of the multiproduct cost function is

$$C(Y,W) = g(Y_1,\ldots,Y_m; W_1,\ldots,W_n) \quad (1)$$

for n inputs and m outputs where the Y_i are output levels and the W_j are input prices. This cost function is the unique dual to the production transformation

$$f(Y_1,\ldots,Y_m; X_1,\ldots,X_n) = 0 \quad (2)$$

(where the X_i are input levels) provided the production structure in expression (2) has a strictly convex input structure (see Fuss and McFadden 1978). This convex input structure is equivalent to the cost function given in expression (1) above, being homogeneous of degree one, nondecreasing, and concave in input prices.

Economies of scope are said to exist in the production of m commodities if the minimized costs of producing given quantities of the goods are less than the combined costs of producing each good separately, i.e., if

$$C(Y_1,\ldots,Y_m; W) < C(Y_1,0,\ldots,0; W) + \ldots + C(0,\ldots,0,Y_m; W); \quad (3)$$
$$Y_1,\ldots,Y_m > 0.$$

The degree of economies of scope is then given by

$$S_C = [C(Y_1,0,\ldots,0; W) + \ldots + C(0,\ldots,0,Y_m; W) - C(Y_1,\ldots,Y_m; W)]/C(Y_1,\ldots,Y_m; W). \quad (4)$$

Willig (1979) and Panzar and Willig (1977, 1978) have shown that a measure of overall returns to scale for a multiproduct firm is given by

$$S = C(Y,W) / \sum_{i=1}^{m} Y_i \frac{\partial C(Y,W)}{\partial Y_i}. \quad (5)$$

Overall returns to scale are therefore increasing, decreasing, or constant as the revenues from pricing outputs at their marginal costs fall short of, exceed, or equal the costs of production. In addition to overall returns to scale, multiproduct firms are subject to product-specific returns to scale which refer to scale economies associated with a particular product line. We first define average incremental costs for product line i which are the per unit costs of adding Y_i units of output to the other outputs and are given by

$$AIC_i = [C(Y,W) - C(Y_1,\ldots,Y_{i-1},0,Y_{i+1},\ldots,Y_m,W]/Y_i. \qquad (6)$$

Product-specific returns to scale in product line i are then defined in the traditional sense as the ratio of average to marginal costs

$$S_i = AIC_i/(\partial C(Y,W)/ Y_i). \qquad (7)$$

Consider now the choice of an explicit representation for the cost function in expression (1). Currently popular multiplicative (or log-additive) cost functions such as the translog are inappropriate for our purposes since they do not permit zero values for any of the firm's outputs. In addition to ruling out the data set used in this study (which includes zero levels of some outputs), the restriction also prohibits the evaluation of economies of scope.[2] On the other hand, strictly additive functional forms which permit zero output levels and the evaluation of economies of scope are difficult to restrict to be linearly homogeneous in input prices. This result in conjunction with the fact that scale and scope characteristics refer to relationships in output space have prompted some authors to suggest an additive function of outputs alone. Baumol and Braunstein (1977) use the following cost function

$$C(Y) = b_0 + \Sigma b_i Y_i + \Sigma\Sigma b_{ij} Y_i Y_j.$$

Baumol, Fischer, and Nadiri (1979) propose the cost function

$$C(Y) = a_0 + (\sum_{1}^{m} (Y_i/a_i)^{\beta})^{1/\alpha\beta}, \quad a_0 \geq 0.$$

Neither of these cost functions has factor prices included explicitly, and thus neither is consistent with duality theory. Omitting factor prices is most likely attributable to the difficulty of having a specification which is both additive in ouputs (required for economies of scope and subadditivity) and homogeneous of degree one in input prices.

Examples of cost functions that are linearly homogeneous in input prices and capable of being tested for economies of scope and subadditivity are the input-output separable functions of Hasenkamp (1973). Hasenkamp combined the constant-elasticity-of-substitution output function of $g(Y) = (\Sigma\delta_i Y_i^{c})^{1/c}$ with both Cobb-Douglas and constant-elasticity-of-substitution input functions. Unfortunately, the functional forms used by Hasenkamp are not flexible and constrain the cost structure to be input-output separable with Allen partial elasticities of substitution equal to one.

The cost function employed here is discussed in more detail in Pulley and Braunstein (1982) and is based on an approximation to the cost function which is dual to a general homothetic, input-output-separable structure:

$$C(Y,W) = g(Y_1,\ldots,Y_m)\ h(W_1,\ldots,W_n). \tag{8}$$

(For a complete discussion of duality in cost and production structures see Fuss and McFadden (1978) and Laitinen (1980).) The output function $g(\cdot)$ is approximated by a second-order Taylor-series expansion. For the input price function $h(\cdot)$ a first-order, log-Taylor-series expansion is used. Therefore:

$$C(y,w) = (\alpha_0 + \sum_i^m \alpha_i Y_i + 1/2 \sum_i^m \sum_j^m \alpha_{ij} Y_i Y_j)(\pi_i^n W_i^{\beta i}) \qquad \text{where } \sum_i^n \beta_i = 1. \tag{8a}$$

The Baumol and Braunstein function above is now seen as being essentially the same as $g(Y_1,Y_2)$. Leaving input prices out of the specification can be interpreted in view of expression (8a) as restrictively implying that

$$\pi_i^n W_i^{\beta i}$$

maintains some constant value, i.e., that input prices change only in a very special way--as determined by the input price parameters.

Unfortunately, the cost function in expression (8a) does not satisfy the requirements of "flexible" functional forms and constrains the production structure to be homothetic as well as input-output separable. It also constrains the Allen partial elasticities of substitution to be unity.[3] These are, of course, significant simplifications: separability, for example, implies that the mix of outputs can be chosen independently of the mix of inputs, i.e., no specific interaction exists between any particular input and any particular output. Unless theory suggests some justification for these restrictions, they should be framed as testable propositions. Therefore, second-order price-output interaction terms were added to the cost function in expression (8a) to obtain the flexible form:

$$C(Y,W) = (\alpha_0 + \sum_i^m \alpha_i Y_i + {}^1/_2 \sum_i^m \sum_j \alpha_{ij} Y_i Y_j + \sum_i^m \sum_j^n \gamma_{ij} Y_i \ln W_j)(\pi_i^n W_i^{\beta i}). \tag{9}$$

This function is linearly homogeneous in input prices when:

$$\sum_i^n \beta_i = 1 \quad \text{and} \quad \sum_j^n \gamma_{ij} = 0 \quad \forall\ i.$$

In the next section, the cost function in expression (9) will be used to investigate the effects of automation on scope and scale economies.

DATA AND RESULTS

The data consist of monthly observations for the period 1973-1980 from a firm in the information sector whose outputs are abstracts of articles in technical journals. The firm produces three separate indices of abstracts. In addition to a large general index, it produces two smaller indices of abstracts relating to more specific topics. These two smaller indices are aggregated to form the second output. (The firm did not begin producing either of the smaller indices until April 1974. The number of abstracts in the monthly indices is used to measure each output.)

Monthly expenditures for five input categories are indentified and included in total costs: (1) total salaries and benefits, (2) printing and binding expenditures, (3) mailing and handling costs, (4) office rent, and (5) production or data processing. Explicit price series for five inputs were developed in the following way. The monthly labor price corresponding to salaries and benefits is obtained by dividing yearly salaries and benefits by the number of full-time-equivalent employees and assuming twelve equal payments. Printing and binding costs are assumed to follow yearly average wages in that industry (SIC Industry Number 2751, Source: Bureau of Labor Statistics). Postal rates for one pound of second-class postage are used as an appropriate price series for mailing and handling (Source: U.S. Postal Service). Monthly rental rates (per square foot) were available from the firm. Production processing costs are assumed to follow yearly average wages in the computer services and data processing industry (SIC Industry Number 737, Source: Bureau of Labor Statistics). All dollar variables were deflated by the GNP deflator and all variables were scaled by their means.

Assuming additive errors, the cost function in expression (9) was estimated using single-equation nonlinear least squares. If, in addition, the errors are assumed to be normally distributed, the coefficients are maximum likelihood estimates. It would have been possible to exploit Sheppard's Lemma and estimate a system of n expenditures equations although, as discussed in Pulley and Braunstein (1982), estimation may be difficult since the system is highly nonlinear in parameters. However, as Guilkey and Lovell (1980) have shown for the translog specification, a single-equation approach may be as promising as estimating the full expenditures-equations model. Since the translog--and our specification as well--are approximations to the true function, a type of specification error is committed in truncating after the second-order terms. Therefore, estimating additional equations may not increase the efficiency of the estimates.[4]

Column I of Table 1 presents coefficient estimates for the cost function in expression (9). Some comments on the assumptions underlying the coefficient estimates in Table 1 are necessary before proceeding. Use of the function in expression (9) implies the assumption of cost-minimizing behavior with respect to each of the five inputs, i.e., the cost function implies an essentially long-run adjustment process. Is it unreasonable to assume that this adjustment process takes place in one month? Certainly, as a general rule, this is not a valid assumption. However, most of this firm's inputs are hired on a fee-for-service basis and can be varied extremely rapidly. Since the firm's outputs (abstracts) depend on the

Table 1

Cost Function Parameter Estimates
(standard errors are given in parentheses)

Coefficient	Full Model I	$S_i=1$ II	Observations 1-48 III	Observations 49-96 IV
α_0	.488 (.185)	.486 (.063)	.395 (.014)	1.26 (.213)
α_1	.402 (.527)	.476 (.070)	.599 (.018)	-.141 (.228)
α_2	.512 (.203)	.447 (.069)	.088 (.035)	-.203 (.136)
α_{12}	-.389 (.229)	-.393 (.068)	-.069 (.036)	.211 (.131)
α_{11}	.076 (.740)	---	---	---
α_{22}	-.071 (.172)	---	---	---
β_1	.396 (.670)	.371 (.671)	.337 (.188)	-10.3 (1.44)
β_2	-3.28 (.805)	-3.07 (.691)	-6.31 (.354)	9.85 (.766)
β_3	-1.13 (.215)	-1.12 (.210)	-.011 (.257)	-.130 (.184)
β_4	-.062 (.366)	.055 (.315)	-.020 (.065)	.351 (.249)
β_5	5.08 (.830)	4.76 (.252)	7.00 (.353)	1.22 (1.13)
γ_{11}	.460 (.464)	.499 (.474)	.576 (.123)	9.65 (2.17)
γ_{12}	1.99 (.604)	2.09 (.521)	5.42 (.268)	-9.35 (1.14)
γ_{13}	.929 (.178)	.970 (.171)	.015 (.167)	.250 (.247)
γ_{14}	.319 (.172)	.304 (.183)	.024 (.031)	-.511 (.497)
γ_{15}	-3.70 (1.42)	-3.86 (.156)	-6.04 (.211)	-.027 (1.79)
γ_{21}	-1.15 (.294)	-1.14 (.272)	.048 (.106)	-.500 (.567)
γ_{22}	2.94 (.958)	2.57 (.478)	-.065 (.150)	.266 (.629)
γ_{23}	.691 (.189)	.624 (.125)	.020 (.111)	-.031 (.134)
γ_{24}	-.414 (.292)	-.522 (.199)	.037 (.031)	.147 (.267)
γ_{25}	-2.07 (.647)	-1.53 (.135)	-.040 (.134)	.118 (.707)
Sum of Squared Errors	.0425764	.0426688	.0001194	.0027861

number of relevant articles appearing in journals, output decisions are essentially exogenous (an implicit assumption in the estimation of the dual cost function). If the technological opportunity set is known to the firm and if most inputs are continuously variable, long-run cost-minimizing adjustments to exogenously determined output levels need not take much time. (See Pulley and Braunstein (1982) for an examination of this issue.)

Assuming the cost function in Column I of Table 1 to be an essentially long-run function, certain additional anomalies need to be explained. Approximately 48 percent of costs remain if outputs are reduced to zero from their mean levels (and input prices are evaluated at their means). How can this be a long-run result? A possible explanation lies in the concept of long-run fixed costs as defined by Baumol, Panzar, and Willig (1982). These refer to fixed costs that are not reduced even in the long run as long as production is not discontinued. The firm under investigation here can be expected to have significant long-run fixed costs. Outputs are measured by the number of abstracts appearing in the monthly indices of abstracts. The long-run fixed costs are those associated with publishing the monthly indices, which will continue even if they contain very few abstracts (i.e., outputs as measured in our model are close to zero). Such costs can be significant. This also explains why we expect dramatic scale economies. Once the printing and data processing capabilities are in place to publish a monthly index, outputs measured by the number of abstracts in these indices should be subject to tremendous apparent economies of scale. These expectations are borne out by the calculations reported below.

Finally, we note that the individual price coefficients in Table 1 are suspect. (Whether the input price structure is adequately modeled is a separate issue.) As described above, appropriate price series for some of the inputs were difficult to obtain and are probably unreliable. This fact in conjunction with the anticipated multicollinearity in time-series observations for five (deflated) price variables helps to explain why the price and price-output coefficients are highly volatile. In fact, some of the input demand equations for the model are negative when evaluated at the variable means. Whether this results from the measurement problems in the price variables, difficulties in capturing the individual characteristics of the input price structure of this particular firm, or inherent difficulties with the functional form in expression (9) has not been investigated. However, our interest in this study is with interactions and relationships in "output space" rather than those specific to inputs or input prices. And, based on the analysis here and in Pulley and Braunstein (1982), we find the observed relationships to be very robust indeed.

Estimates of economies of scope and overall as well as product-specific returns to scale are easily determined for the mean values of the scaled variables since the mean variables of the scaled variables are all one. For the model in Column I of Table 1:

$$A\hat{I}C_1 = \hat{\alpha}_1 + \hat{\alpha}_{12} + {}^1/2\hat{\alpha}_{11} \tag{10}$$

$$A\hat{I}C_2 = \hat{\alpha}_2 + \hat{\alpha}_{12} + {}^1/2\hat{\alpha}_{22} \tag{11}$$

$$\hat{S}_1 = A\hat{I}C_1/\hat{\alpha}_1 + \hat{\alpha}_{12} + \hat{\alpha}_{11}) = (\hat{\alpha}_1 + \hat{\alpha}_{12} + {}^1/2\hat{\alpha}_{11})/(\hat{\alpha}_1 + \hat{\alpha}_{12} + \hat{\alpha}_{11}) \tag{12}$$

$$\hat{S}_2 = A\hat{I}C_2/\hat{\alpha}_2 + \hat{\alpha}_{12} + \hat{\alpha}_{22}) = (\hat{\alpha}_2 + \hat{\alpha}_{12} + {}^1/2\hat{\alpha}_{22})/(\hat{\alpha}_2 + \hat{\alpha}_{12} + \hat{\alpha}_{22}) \tag{13}$$

$$\hat{S} = \frac{\hat{\alpha}_0 + \hat{\alpha}_1 + \hat{\alpha}_2 + \hat{\alpha}_{12} + {}^1/2\hat{\alpha}_{11} + {}^1/2\hat{\alpha}_{22}}{\hat{\alpha}_1 + \hat{\alpha}_2 + 2\hat{\alpha}_{12} + \hat{\alpha}_{11} + \hat{\alpha}_{22}} \tag{14}$$

$$\hat{S}_c = \frac{\hat{\alpha}_0 - \hat{\alpha}_{12}}{\hat{\alpha}_0 + \hat{\alpha}_1 + \hat{\alpha}_2 + \hat{\alpha}_{12} + {}^1/2\hat{\alpha}_{11} + {}^1/2\hat{\alpha}_{22}} \tag{15}$$

Assuming normally distributed errors so that the coefficient estimates are maximum-likelihood estimates, a method for determining (approximate) asymptotic standard errors for the estimators above is given in the appendix.

Column I of Table 2 presents estimates of $A\hat{I}C_1$, $A\hat{I}C_2$, $\hat{S}_1$, $\hat{S}_2$, $\hat{S}$, and $\hat{S}_C$ for the full model in Column I of Table 1 when variables take their mean values. The nature of outputs (abstracts) and the scale economies that may reasonably be assumed to exist in production processing and printing and binding activities would lead us to expect the firm under consideration to display considerable scale economies. Also, since many of the abstracts in the general index appear in edited form in one of the smaller indices and since many of the inputs the firm employs in the production of one output are costlessly available to and valuable in the production of the other output, i.e., are public in the sense of Panzar and Willig (1978), the firm should exhibit scope economies as well. The values in Column I of Table 2 indicate considerable scale and scope economies. For example, the value of 0.86 for economies of scope indicates that the costs of producing the mean values of the two outputs separately would be 86 percent greater than the costs of producing them jointly.

Product-specific returns to scale, economies of scope, and overall returns to scale are related in the following way (Willig 1979):

$$S = \frac{V_1 S_1 + V_2 S_2}{1 - S_C} \quad \text{where} \quad V_i = \frac{Y_i \partial C(Y,W)/\partial Y_i}{\sum_j^m Y_j \partial C(Y,W)/\partial Y_j}$$

Therefore, although product-specific returns to scale are not significantly different from unity, the large scope economies contribute to the potential for overall scale economies.

Column II of Table 1 presents the results of estimating the model when product-specific returns to scale are constrained to be unity, i.e., when the (statistically insignificant) coefficients on the squared output terms are constrained to zero. The standard errors of the output coefficients are greatly reduced, presumably due to the reduction in multicollinearity. To determine the appropriateness of the model in Column II of Table 1 an asymptotic likelihood ratio test was performed. The test value of 0.2 was well within the 0.10-level critical value for $\chi^2(2)$ of 4.6. Therefore, the model in Column II of Table 1 will be adopted in further analysis.

Column II of Table 2 presents the values of $A\hat{I}C_i$, $\hat{S}_i$, $\hat{S}$, and $\hat{S}_C$ for the model in Column II of Table 1. The values of the unrestricted properties of the production structure are virtually identical to those obtained for the full model, but the standard errors are generally much smaller.

The values in the first two columns of Table 2 describe the properties of the cost and production structure for this firm over the entire eight-year period (1973-1980). Our interest here, however, concerns how these properties were affected by the switch to computerized production processing in

Table 2

Scale and Scope Economies
(asymptotic standard errors are in parentheses)

Relevant Model from Table 2	Full Model I	$S_i=1$ II	Observations I-48 III	Observations 49-96 IV
AIC_1	.051 (.363)	.083 (.055)	.530 (.030)	.071 (.118)
AIC_2	.088 (.084)	.054 (.018)	.019 (.019)	.008 (.045)
S_1	.574 (2.89)	1	1	1
S_2	1.67 (5.99)	1	1	1
S	7.17 (2.45)	7.41 (2.50)	1.85 (.123)	14.3 (17.9)
S_c	.863 (.391)	.865 (.045)	.458 (.032)	.930 (.089)

the early years of the period. The general approach of including a time variable with appropriate second-order interaction terms is most likely unwarranted in this application. In fact, initial attempts to incorporate a shift or time variable explicitly into the cost function led to exactly the situation as depicted in Fig. 2. When evaluated at current or mean output levels, the derivative of the cost function with respect to time was positive. When evaluated at significantly larger output values, the derivative was negative. The function also exhibited large scope and scale economies similar to those reported in Table 2.

While there is enough information available to rule out use of time or shift variables, there is not enough information to suggest a means for explicitly modeling the changes in the production structure. Therefore, the following procedure was adopted. The cost function in Column I of Table 1 was estimated over the two subperiods 1973-1976 and 1977-1980. (Coefficient values are contained in Columns III and IV of Table 1.) Values of $\hat{AIC}_i$, $\hat{S}_i$, $\hat{S}$, and $\hat{S}c$ were then computed from the coefficients for each of the two models using the mean values of the variables for the entire eight-year period to facilitate comparisons. (The variables were not rescaled for each subperiod.) These values are contained in Columns III and IV of Table 2.

As expected due to the scale and scope advantages which this sort of automation should introduce, the values of economies of scale and scope are considerably larger in the latter period. Furthermore, there is some indication, albeit not very reliable, that average incremental costs were reduced by the switch to computer processing as well. (Since the second output is smaller and contains many re-edited entries from the first output, average incremental costs appear to be smaller for it and are affected less by the automation.)

By automating its data processing, retrieval, and editing tasks, the firm has apparently gained for itself significant scale and scope economies and has perhaps reduced the costs of expanding either product line separately. The observation of the managers that the change seemed most appropriate in anticipation of future expansion is borne out by our analysis. Whether the result holds for other firms in the rapidly expanding information sector or for automation in general awaits the findings of additional inquiry.

SUMMARY AND CONCLUSIONS

Whether referred to as technological change, technical change, productivity growth, or progress, the process by which efficient production structures and opportunity sets change over time raises interesting questions. Unfortunately no generally applicable empirical technique for monitoring the progress has been developed. Certainly part of the problem is definitional. Exactly what is meant by productivity growth? (See Caves, Christensen, and Swanson 1981.) However, much of the problem is operational. Technological change however defined is--like the production process itself--specific to the firm or industry under analysis. In this vein, we have endeavored to allow firm-specific information to shape our approach as well as the area of focus.

NOTES

The authors gratefully acknowledge research suppport from the Division of Information Science and Technology of the National Science Foundation.

1 Quite frankly, they also mentioned as another justification the "bandwagon effect" or the notion that "everyone seems to be automating."

2 Caves, Christensen, and Tretheway (1980) have generalized the translog function to allow for zero output values. Their generalization is obtained by substituting for Y_i in the translog function the expression $(Y_i^\lambda-1)/\lambda$ which has $\ln Y_i$ as its limit (as $\lambda \to 0$). Unfortunately, as pointed out in Pulley and Braunstein (1982), this specification remains inappropriate for examining properties of multiproduct cost and production structures such as subadditivity.

3 In fact, if α_0 and α_{12} are zero, the function is output independent, meaning that the multiproduct firm whose cost function is given by expression (8a) could be broken up into m separable firms and these firms, each independently adjusting outputs and inputs to maximize profits, would use the same aggregate level of each input and produce the same aggregate level of each output as the multiproduct firm (see Laitinen 1980).

4 In a more recent study, Guilkey, Lovell, and Sickles (1981) have revised their conclusions somewhat. "When partial elasticities diverge from each other, and particularly when complementarity is present, the systems estimator shows a clear dominance over the single equation estimator...." Multi-equation estimates using the model in expression (9) are reported in Pulley and Braunstein (1982).

APPENDIX

Let $$\hat{\alpha} = \begin{matrix} \hat{\alpha}_1 \\ \cdot \\ \cdot \\ \cdot \\ \hat{\alpha}_r \end{matrix} \quad \text{and} \quad \alpha = \begin{matrix} \alpha_1 \\ \cdot \\ \cdot \\ \cdot \\ \alpha_r \end{matrix}$$ be the vector of coefficient

estimates and their expected values for the model in expression (9) above. [α as used here is not to be confused with α as it appears in expression (9).] Since, under our assumptions, α is a vector of maximum-likelihood estimates, the estimator $n^{1/2}$ $(\hat{\alpha} - \alpha)$ has a normal limiting distribution with zero mean vector and variance matrix equal to $n\Sigma$ [where Σ is the inverse of the information matrix with terms which are $O(n^{-1})$]. Consider a function $S(\hat{\alpha})$. If $S(\hat{\alpha})$ has continuous second-order derivatives in some region that contains α as an interior point, it can be proved (Thiel 1971, chapter 8, especially problems 3.1-3.3, 3.6, 3.7) that $n^{1/2}$ $[S(\alpha) - S(\alpha)]$ has a limiting normal distribution with zero mean and variance $ns'\Sigma s$ where s is the gradient of $S(\cdot)$ evaluated at α. Thus, $S(\alpha)$ is asymptotically normal with mean $S(\alpha)$ and variance $s'\Sigma s$. Since both Σ and s are functions of the unknown vector α, but are evaluated at $\hat{\alpha}$, the values in parentheses in Table 2 are asymptotic errors.

Actually, the values in Table 2 are also functions of the sample values. Therefore, no simple statements can be made concerning their asymptotic distribution. [See Anderson and Thursby (1982) for an analysis of this problem.] The standard errors in Table 2 can, at best, be viewed as approximations.

REFERENCES

1 Anderson, R.G. and Thursby, J.G., Some Evidence on the Distribution of Elasticity Estimators in Translog Models, Department of Economics, Ohio State University, mimeo (1982).

2 Baumol, W.J. and Braunstein, Y.M., Empirical study of scale economies and product complementarity: The case of journal publication, Journal of Political Economy 85 (1977) 1037-1048.

3 Baumol, W.J.; Fischer, D.; and Nadiri, M.I., Forms for Empirical Cost Functions to Evaluate Efficiency of Industry Structure, New York University Economic Discussion Paper 79-18 (1979).

4 Baumol, W.J.; Panzar, J.; and Willig, R., Contestable Markets and the Theory of Market Structure (Harcourt Brace Jovanovich, New York, 1982).

5 Caves, D.W.; Christensen, L.R.; and Swanson, J.A., Productivity growth, scale economies, and capacity utilization in U.S. railroads, 1955-74, American Economic Review 71, 5 (1981) 994-1002.

6 Caves, D.W.; Christensen, L.R.; and Tretheway, M.W., Flexible cost functions for multiproduct firms, Review of Economics and Statistics (August 1980) 477-481.

7 Fuss, M. and McFadden, D. (eds.), Production Economics: A Dual Approach to Theory and Application, volume I, The Theory of Production (North-Holland, Amsterdam, 1978).

8 Guilkey, D.K. and Lovell, C.A.K., On the flexibility of the Translog Approximation, International Economic Review 21, 1 (1980) 137-147.

9 Guilkey, D.K.; Lovell, C.A.K.; and Sickles, R., A Comparison of the Performance of Three Flexible Forms, University of North Carolina, mimeo (1981).

10 Hasenkamp, G., A study of multi-output production functions, Journal of Econometrics 4 (1973) 253.

11 Laitinen, K., A Theory of the Multiproduct Firm (North-Holland, Amsterdam, 1980).

12 Panzar, J. and Willig, R.D., Economies of scale in multi-output production, Quarterly Journal of Economics 91 (1977) 481-494.

13 Panzar, J. and Willig, R.D., Economies of Scope, Product Specific Economies of Scale, and Multiproduct Competitive Industries, Unpublished paper, Bell Laboratories (1978).

14 Pulley, L.B and Braunstein, Y.M., Multiproduct Cost Functions: An Empirical Investigation, Brandeis Working Paper No. 81-105 (1982).

15 Stevenson, R., Measuring technological bias, American Economic Review 70, 1 (1980) 162-173.

16 Thiel, H., Principles of Econometrics (John Wiley and Sons, New York, 1971).

17 Willig, R.D., Multiproduct technology and market structure, American Economic Review: Papers and Proceedings 69, 2 (1979) 346-351.

COMMUNICATION AND INFORMATION ECONOMICS:
New Perspectives
M. Jussawalla and H. Ebenfield (Editors)

A GROWTH MODEL OF THE U.S. COMMUNICATION INDUSTRY, 1948-80

Nestor E. Terleckyj

I. INTRODUCTION

Objectives and Content of the Report

The communication sector is one of the main sources of strength of the American economy. Long a source of basic technologies, it is now evolving linked to computer use and computer technology. The rapid growth of communication output and productivity contributes not only to overall economic growth directly but also to the growth in output and productivity of other sectors. Far beyond this, the growth and spread of these technologies is likely to change the nature of modern economies by the end of this century, perhaps justifying the term "information economy" in the sense that most work performed will deal with production, processing, storing, interpretation and distribution of information.

This paper reports the results of a project concerned with the dynamics of growth of the communication sector and its contributions to the growth of the economy. The main objective of this project has been to increase the understanding of the dynamics of the growth of the communications sector and of the mechanism and the sources which have contributed to its strength consistently over the years. To this end, a consistent dynamic growth model of the communication sector was to be developed that could describe the relationships among labor and capital inputs, research and development (R&D), productivity, output, price of, and demand for communication. Ultimately the research reported here is intended to help explore the interactions between communication and the rest of the economy and to examine the contributions of computers and of communication inputs to growth of the American economy.

The analyses presented here build on previous research in the economics of technical change. However, the communication sector is much more technology-intensive than the rest of the economy. This is made clear by the amounts of private and government R&D spending, which are much higher relative to output in communication (9.3 percent in 1980) than in the business economy as a whole (2.8 percent).

Compared to the highly diversified output of the U.S. economy, the output of the communication sector is relatively homogenous. It consists of transmission of information through various channels. The bulk of the measured output of the communication sector consists of production of telecommunication message units. The output of communication is measured much more accurately than is the output of the economy as a whole. Hence, it may be possible to observe in this sector at least some of the economic processes of technical change with greater clarity and in greater detail than is possible in most other industries, or at the macroeconomic level.

The results obtained may be helpful in increasing the understanding of the contributions of other high technology sectors to the process of economic growth.

While there have been specialized econometric studies of productivity change in the telecommunication industry (e.g., Nadiri and Shankerman 1980), there have been no comprehensive studies of growth from both the demand and supply side of the communication sector and of its impact on the economy. Further, the role of government expenditure for R&D in stimulating private investments in communication R&D and in generating productivity increases in the communication sector have not been examined before. The time dimension of the relationships between government R&D, private R&D, and productivity change in communication have not been previously explored empirically. Finally, no complete model of growth of the communication sector was previously estimated. These subjects are the main concern of the research reported here. Another innovation of the present analysis is the attempt to introduce computer use into the estimation of an economic growth model.

Theoretical Formulation

The theoretical model of the communication sector underlying the present analysis is drawn from previous research in the fields of economics of R&D and productivity change. Private industry R&D expenditures are treated as investment on par with fixed investment. This economic model involves a concept of a production function of labor and capital, changing under the impact of accumulation of R&D capital. Specific theoretical assumptions of this model, such as the neutrality of technical change induced by the R&D capital input are tested explicitly, and the model is modified to accommodate the results of these tests.

Several empirical relationships are estimated and analyzed here. First, an investment equation for private R&D expenditures in electrical equipment and communication is derived, based on such variables as the output of the communication sector, the level of economic activity, and the past government expenditures for R&D in electrical equipment and communication (Section II). Next, an econometric model developed for estimating stocks of R&D capital is outlined, and the R&D capital stock is estimated empirically by means of distributed lag analyses from R&D to total factor productivity (Section III). Then a production function is estimated in which the stocks of past private (and government) R&D expenditures enter as inputs, along with labor and the fixed capital stock in the production of the communication sector output (Section IV). The relative price of the communication output is estimated as a function of relative total factor productivity of communication and of the fixed capital stock ratio reflecting, presumably, regulatory behavior (Section V). Demand equation for output of communication includes relative price of communication output and the income of the economy (GNP). The number of computers used in the economy is also included in the analysis on an experimental basis (Section VI). An overview of the resulting growth model estimated for the communication sector is provided in Section VII.

The individual relationships of this model are clearly interdependent in that the dependent variables of each equation are also explanatory variables in at least one other relationship. Beyond the development of a partial growth model of the communication sector there are possibilities of integrating this model of the communication sector or its later version with the analysis of growth of the economy as a whole. However, the relationship of the communication sector to the growth of the economy cannot be pursued within the scope of this study.

The Data

Relatively long time series are required for the analysis of growth of the communication sector. The basic period of analysis is 1948-80. However, because of the time lags among the variables, some data series, in particular the R&D expenditure data, had to be extended to earlier years.

The choice of the subject material and the decision to estimate a complete growth model for the communication sector dictates certain choices of data, of the level of industry aggregation, and of the research strategies. Because the multi-equation system analyzed here involves a fairly large number of variables, it can be identified consistently only at the level of the communication sector as a whole. This sector includes the telecommunication industry as well as television and radio broadcasting and related services. By choosing this level of aggregation, certain inadequacies in the data base are accepted. While output and prices are measured relatively well for the telecommunication industry, they are not measured nearly as well for broadcasting and related services. However, a complete set of long-term data series for variables such as prices, capital stocks, and especially the R&D expenditure is not available separately for the telecommunication industry. Hence, most of the analyses have to be conducted at the level of the total communication sector. The R&D data used relates to the more aggregate, but overlapping, category of electrical equipment and communication.

The output, man-hours, price, and labor compensation data used in the present analysis are the Bureau of Labor Statistics, Business Sector data (1981 data base). The total factor productivity data used to estimate the embodiment period for the R&D expenditures were developed by Elliot S. Grossman and John W. Kendrick at the American Productivity Center and were provided by the courtesy of the authors. The fixed capital investment and fixed capital stock data are also obtained from Grossman and Kendrick.

The private R&D expenditure series used in this paper is shown in Table 1 for the years 1921-80. It is based on the company-funded expenditure for research and development in communication and electrical equipment industries compiled by the NSF for the years 1953-1980. The series is extended back to 1927 and then extrapolated back to 1921 based on benchmark data from other sources as described in the note to Table 1.

The corresponding data for the government-funded R&D in electrical equipment and communication industries is shown in Table 2. The R&D capital stocks analyzed in this paper are compounded from these R&D expenditure series in accordance with the estimating procedures discussed in the next section.

Table 1

Estimates of Company Expenditure for Performance of R&D
In Electrical Equipment and Communication Industries, 1921-80
(in millions of 1972 dollars)

Year	Expenditure	Year	Expenditure
1921	$ 115	1951	$ 570
1922	124	1952	617
1923	133	1953	667
1924	143	1954	736
1925	154	1955	804
1926	166	1956	870
1927	178	1957	936
1928	182	1958	957
1929	196	1959	1018
1930	191	1960	1233
1931	195	1961	1279
1932	200	1962	1344
1933	204	1963	1419
1934	209	1964	1502
1935	214	1965	1622
1936	219	1966	1842
1937	224	1967	1963
1938	229	1968	2119
1939	234	1969	2255
1940	240	1970	2196
1941	259	1971	2219
1942	280	1972	2313
1943	303	1973	2357
1944	328	1974	2353
1945	355	1975	2228
1946	384	1976	2332
1947	416	1977	2316
1948	450	1978	2484
1949	487	1979	2771
1950	527	1980	3039

SOURCES: Current dollar data for company-funded R&D performance in communication and electrical equipment industries for 1953-80 were obtained from the NSF Research and Development Industry report. The current dollar data were converted to 1972 dollars by the GNP deflator. The series was extended to earlier years using benchmark data for R&D employment in electrical equipment and communication industries in 1952, 1940, and 1927 from an earlier study (Terleckyj 1963, 109). The 1952 employment was attributed to government and private funding in proportion to expenditures reported for 1953. The 1940 employment was attributed to company funding. The constant dollar data for intervening years was interpolated by a growth rate of 8.2 percent from 1940 to 1953 and a rate of 2.3 percent from 1927 to 1940. Extension to 1921 was based on estimated changes in total private R&D expenditure (Terleckyj 1982).

Table 2

Estimates of Federal Government Expenditure for Performance of R&D In Electrical Equipment and Communication Industries, 1939-80 (in millions of 1972 dollars)

Year	Expenditure	Year	Expenditure
1939	$ 0	1961	$ 2302
1940	11	1962	2395
		1963	2580
1941	69	1964	2553
1942	137	1965	2640
1943	230		
1944	328	1966	2831
1945	378	1967	2841
		1968	2826
1946	329	1969	2754
1947	264	1970	2418
1948	274		
1949	298	1971	2351
1950	310	1972	2367
		1973	2280
1951	325	1974	2007
1952	454	1975	1837
1953	787		
1954	875	1976	1934
1955	963	1977	1930
		1978	1909
1956	1050	1979	2095
1957	1842	1980	2103
1958	2025		
1959	2429		
1960	2438		

SOURCES: Data for government-funded performance in electrical equipment and communication industries were obtained from selected issues of the NSF Research and Development in Industry report. That series was extended back to 1940 by percentage changes in a series representing a Department of Defense estimate of total government-funded R&D performed in industry published in Long-Term Economic Growth 1860-1970 (U.S. Department of Commerce). The resulting current dollar series was converted to 1972 dollars by the GNP deflator.

The Statistical Approach

The statistical results reported here are generally based on generalized least squares (GLS) estimates of the equations specified in the individual sections of this analysis. The advantage of generalized least squares (GLS) estimation is that the hypothesis tests are not biased by the autocorrelation in the residuals. The GLS estimates are tested for consistency with alternate estimates, specifically, the ordinary least squares (OLS), and with the estimates made by the robust techniques, i.e., the least absolute error (LAE) and the biweighted least squares (BWLS) including their autoregressive iterative transformation procedures (Levy 1983). Differences in the results obtained with the different estimating methods are reported where they are important.

The advantage of the robust technique estimation is that in cases where the distribution of residuals is not normal, the weight given to outlying observations is much less than in the least squares estimates and the distortion in the parameter estimates is much reduced. The use of ordinary least squares (OLS) in lieu of constrained least squares has the advantage of involving fewer additional assumptions; in particular, the OLS techniques lend themselves to the estimation of some of the distributed lag structures made here.

Periods of Analysis

The statistical estimates are made for the period 1948-80. All estimates are replicated systematically, where possible, for two subperiods, 1948-63 and 1964-80, or for the later subperiod alone. The subperiod estimates are made to examine changes in the various relationships over time. Some data, in particular the R&D data, are more reliable for the later years than for the earlier part of the period. Hence, the estimates made for the later period may be more reliable and should, therefore, receive greater weight.

There are substantive reasons for examining the stability of economic relationships over these particular subperiods. Communication technology changed radically by the introduction of satellites in the early 1960s, the competitive environment of the industry had changed materially. Before the mid-1960s, communication technology was changing within a rather stable industry organization structure consisting, for the most part, of regulated telephone utilities with a large market share of one company. During the 1960s, the interaction between computer use and communication began. The number of companies manufacturing telecommunication equipment and the nature of the technologies involved changed. The industry became more diversified, and the number of participants, especially suppliers of technology and equipment, including foreign suppliers, greatly increased. By 1983 the federal deregulation became complete. The largest telephone utilities were separated from equipment manufacturing, and supply of equipment was opened to interindustry and international competition.

Some of the trends for the basic economic indicators of the industry changed during the 1960s. The decline in the share of compensation of labor in the total value-added produced by the industry ended, and the labor share began to rise after 1964. Also the price of the output of the communication industry relative to the price of the total output of the private business sector was stable until 1963; the relative price of communication declined sharply after 1963. As is evident from the results presented in this report, most of the relationships estimated for the communication industry differed substantially between these two subperiods.

II. INVESTMENT IN RESEARCH AND DEVELOPMENT

Expenditure for research and development by private industry is a form of business investment. The level of private investment in R&D is determined by many of the same factors that influence the expenditure for plant and equipment. These are the level of output of the economy, corporate taxes, unemployment, and the age of the relevant capital stocks. The impact of these factors on the level of different types of investment varies (Terleckyj, Holdrich, and Levy 1982).

There is, however, one distinct and important factor that influences private investment in R&D. It is the amount of government expenditure for R&D. According to a recent joint study by the author (Levy and Terleckyj 1983), the available evidence indicates that, economy-wide, a dollar of government expenditure for R&D performed under contract in industry has been associated statistically with 27 cents of private industry R&D expenditure. There is also some indication that government-funded R&D performed in universities and in government also may have a positive effect on private R&D spending, but this relationship is much more uncertain.

A number of studies conducted independently over the past several years have consistently found evidence of positive association between government R&D and private R&D at the level of industries, companies and products. (Goldberg 1979; Levin and Rice 1981; Link 1982; Mansfield and Switzer 1982; Scott 1981). Typically, the size of the estimated effects of government R&D on private R&D spending found in these studies was smaller than the coefficients obtained at the macroeconomic level. One possible reason is that the microeconomic estimates do not reflect the interindustry, intercompany, interproduct effects of government R&D on private R&D which are outside their scope. It is plausible that performance of research and development under contract for the government results in development of a product which may be converted by the same company or by another company through additional, privately funded R&D into a product to be used in the private sector. It is also plausible that such private market adaptations lead to further R&D activities aimed at developing imitations, competing and complementary products and complementary processes. Much of this derived privately funded R&D may be performed in industries, companies, or product fields different from those of the original government contract.

It is also plausible that at least some of this derived private R&D would follow the original government R&D with a lag of some years. In some of the studies cited, evidence was obtained that the relationship between government R&D and the private R&D expenditures involved lags of several years. Other studies that addressed this issue did not find evidence of such time lags.

Aside from these questions, there is no a priori reason to expect that the relationship between government R&D and private R&D expenditures be the same in all industries, or that it remain the same over time. Here, both the magnitude and the timing of the statistical relationship between government contract R&D and private R&D in communication and electrical equipment expenditure is analyzed in some subperiod detail.

The following R&D investment equation is estimated:

$$RD_C = a_0 + a_1\, Q_C(-1) + a_2\, U + \sum_{t=-4}^{0} W(t)GRD(t) \qquad \text{(II-1)}$$

in which the amount of private R&D expenditure for electrical equipment and communication, RDc, depends on the level of communication output lagged one year, Qc(-1), on the current business conditions represented by unemployment, U, and on the past levels of government expenditure for contract R&D in electrical equipment and communication, GRDc, lagged four years, with variable effects, wt, of contract R&D performed in each year. The estimates of this equation for the period 1948-80 and the two subperiods using alternately four year distributed Shiller lag structure for government R&D and the government R&D in the year (-2) are shown in Table 3.

The effect of communication output on R&D investment is consistent and is highly significant in all three cases but one. Effect of unemployment is significant only in the second subperiod, in which the recession levels of unemployment were much higher than in the first subperiod.

The estimated effect of government R&D on private R&D in electrical equipment and telecommunication is highly significant. The results also indicate that there has been a time lag in the relation between government R&D and private R&D in this industry. The Shiller lag estimates and the OLS estimates of the corresponding lag structure (not shown in Table 3) had statistically significant coefficients (at at least 5 percent level) in the past years. But the unconstrained OLS estimates contain a large amount of "noise," and the Shiller lag estimates involve prior assumptions about the lag structure and contain large (though not significant) estimates of the regression constant in the second subperiod. The GLS estimates based on government R&D in year (-2) bring out more clearly the underlying relationship between government R&D and private R&D. They produce comparable, but somewhat lower, estimates of the total effects of government R&D in each period analyzed.

The estimates shown in Table 3 also suggest that the effect of government r&d on the private R&D spending has increased substantially between the subperiods, in case of GLS estimates from 10 cents per dollar in the first subperiod to 56 cents in the second, and in the case of the Shiller lag estimates from 17 cents to 76 cents. For the entire period 1948-80, the GLS estimate and the sum of Shiller coefficients are close together at 0.31 and 0.34 and somewhat higher than the 0.27 estimated for the economy, but much higher than any of the previous estimates made at the industry level. While these results appear quite meaningful, more research is required to obtain more definitive estimates of the R&D investment function for communication, especially with regard to the shape of the lag structure for government R&D and its possible shift over time and for the components of the total R&D in electrical equipment and communication.

Additional variables and alternative formulations of the R&D investment equation were investigated, but no additional insights were obtained. The age of R&D stock was not found to be significant for R&D investment in communication. In another analysis, private fixed investment in communication was included in the investment equation for private R&D with the intent of capturing the possible effect of other factors influencing investment in general. But its addition to the equation II-1 did not produce any additional explanation beyond that obtained by government R&D, lagged communication output, and unemployment.

Table 3

Investment Function for Private R&D in Electrical Equipment and Communication
Estimates of the equation:

$$RD_c = a_o + a_1 Q_c(-1) + a_2 U + \sum_{t=-4}^{0} W(t)GRD(t)$$

(in millions of 1972 dollars; t-ratios in parentheses)

Regression Coefficient	Shiller Lag Estimates 1948-80	Shiller Lag Estimates 1948-63	Shiller Lag Estimates 1964-80	CLS Estimates 1948-80	CLS Estimates 1948-63	CLS Estimates 1964-80
a_o	359.49** (7.80)	176.04 (0.60)	-935.91 (1.45)	306.41** (5.35)	-15.42 (0.29)	-362.03 (1.11)
a_1	0.050** (24.73)	0.067 (1.49)	0.053** (7.18)	0.050** (20.62)	0.093** (12.01)	0.054** (15.87)
a_2	-81.37** (5.69)	-15.95 (0.74)	-33.84 (1.00)	-62.63** (3.63)	-15.74 (1.46)	-61.77** (3.08)
w(0)	0.001 (0.02)	-0.001 (0.02)	0.182 (1.11)			
W(-1)	0.063 (1.73)	0.027 (1.17)	0.147 (1.50)			
W(-2)	0.087 (2.00)	0.046 (1.83)	0.161 (1.77)	0.314** (12.92)	0.096** (3.79)	0.560** (5.69)
W(-3)	0.100* (2.77)	0.052 (1.68)	0.178 (1.60)			
W(-4)	0.086 (1.83)	0.046 (0.99)	0.094 (0.84)			
R^2 (Corrected)	0.994	0.998	0.999	0.996	0.999	0.999
D-W Statistic	0.964	2.14	1.47	1.63	2.20	1.86
Sum, Lag Coeffs.	0.337	0.170	0.762	0.314	0.096	0.560

*Statistically significant at 5 percent. **Statistically significant at 1 percent.

III. STOCKS OF R&D CAPITAL IN COMMUNICATION

The Embodiment Lag Model

The results of R&D activities performed in a given year as a rule do not become available for use in production until some years later. Hence, estimation of capital stock of R&D available for production requires lagging of the past R&D expenditure over an appropriate embodiment period. This period includes the time between the average R&D expenditure and the development of the resulting producer-good innovations and the time of diffusion and absorption of these innovations in the industries using them. The length of this period is estimated here empirically.

Until recently, no empirical estimates of the embodiment period of R&D lags were available, except in agriculture, where a long embodiment period of agricultural research in agricultural production was identified (Evenson 1978). Recently, an empirical estimate of the embodiment lag was made by the author for total U.S. private R&D expenditure based on its distributed lag impacts on the private business sector productivity (Terleckyj 1982b). A revised version of this estimating model is developed and applied here to the R&D and productivity data for the communication sector.

The embodiment lag is estimated by extending the marginal product of the R&D capital model, which has been used to estimate the productivity effects of R&D for some time. Recent descriptions of this model were provided by Griliches and Lichtenberg (1982) and Terleckyj (1982a). In this model, output is a Cobb-Douglas production function of labor and capital with an additional disembodied productivity growth trend at the rate λ and a factor-neutral contribution of research capital R given by its own elasticity parameter, α :

$$Q = Ae^{\lambda t}L^{\beta}K^{(1-\beta)}R^{\alpha} \qquad \text{(III-1)}$$

Productivity is defined as follows:

$$P = Q/L^{\beta}K^{(1-\beta)} = Ae^{\lambda t}R \qquad \text{(III-2)}$$

Differentiating this function with respect to time gives the equation for productivity growth in which the growth rate of productivity is the sum of the disembodied autonomous growth term and growth in the stock of R&D capital times the elasticity of output with respect to the R&D capital stock:

$$P = \frac{\dot{P}}{P} = \lambda + \alpha\frac{\dot{R}}{R} \qquad \text{(III-3)}$$

If the depreciation rate for R&D capital is zero (or small enough to be ignored) the elasticity term in equation III-3 can be replaced by a term containing the marginal product of R&D capital as follows:

$$\lambda + \alpha\frac{\dot{R}}{R} = \lambda + \frac{\partial Q}{\partial R} \cdot \frac{R}{Q} \cdot \frac{\dot{R}}{R} = \lambda + \frac{\partial Q}{\partial R} \cdot \frac{\dot{R}}{Q} \tag{III-4}$$

In equation III-4, the growth rate of productivity is specified as the sum of the disembodied term and the marginal product or R&D capital times the ratio of the increment in the R&D capital to output. Recent research results indicate that the depreciation rate of R&D as a factor of production is either zero or small enough to be empirically indistinguishable from zero with the present data, in that statistically stronger results are obtained when zero depreciation rate is assumed than when the depreciation rate is assumed than with the depreciation rate of 10 percent or more (Griliches and Lichtenberg 1982; Terleckyj 1982a). Thus, it appears that while R&D is subject to obsolescence, unlike labor and fixed capital, it does not wear out by use in production and the passage of time, and need not be replaced for those reasons. Hence, it should not be depreciated in productivity analyses, at least not at the relatively high rates of 10, or perhaps even 5 percent. Whether a much lower rate of depreciation, such as 2 percent or less, is more appropriate for industrial R&D than zero cannot be resolved at this time, and no depreciation of R&D is assumed here.

The equation III-4 is static. It does not specify the period over which the R&D expenditures become a part of the R&D capital that is available for production. In the absence of an embodiment lag, the increment in the R&D capital over a time interval would equal the R&D expenditure during this interval. However, the R&D capital resulting from a given R&D expenditure is not immediately available in production. In fact, the results of the research on the diffusion of innovations in agriculture and industry (Griliches 1957; Mansfield 1968, 1977) suggest that the embodiment lags for much of R&D are probably quite long. Because of its length, the embodiment lag of R&D should be recognized explicitly in analyzing production and productivity. To this end the R&D capital stock in period t is specified as follows for discrete periods and assuming no depreciation of R&D:

$$R_t = W_o\, E_t + W_1\, E_{t-1} + \ldots + W_a\, E_{t-a} = \sum_{s=o}^{a} W_s\, E_{t-s} \tag{III-5}$$

Here the coefficients Ws, $0 \leq W_s \leq 1$, represent the proportion of the expenditure, Et-s, of the period (t-s) which had already been embodied in the R&D stock and t-a is the first period in which an R&D expenditure was made. The values of the embodiment coefficients Ws rise cumulatively from zero in the period sufficiently recent so that none of the R&D expenditure is yet embodied in the R&D capital stock, to one in all periods sufficiently far in the past so that the R&D expenditures made in these periods are fully embodied in the R&D capital stock. Because the depreciation rate of R&D capital is assumed to be zero, all past expenditures eventually remain fully embodied in R_t. If a positive depreciation rate were to be assumed, this formulation could be readily adapted to it by addition of the depreciation factors to the series in III-5. The change in the capital stock is then defined as follows:

$$\Delta R_t = R_t - R_{t-1} = \sum_{s=o}^{a} W_s\, E_{t-s} - \sum_{s=o}^{a} W_s\, E_{t-s+1} \tag{III-6}$$

$$= W_0\, E_t + \sum_{s=o}^{a} (W_s - W_{s-1})E_{t-s}$$

Here the changes in the capital R&D stock over the interval from t-1 to t is the weighted sum of current and past R&D expenditures with the weights, $v_s = W_x W_s - 1$ given by the differences in the embodiment coefficients for the successive past periods. For the current period t, the weight v_0 equals the embodiment coefficient W_0. The positive values of the weights v_s are contained in a finite time interval representing an embodiment period of length a, and zero values otherwise. These weights can be estimated statistically by specifying a dynamic version of the equation III-4 assuming that the marginal product of R&D capital is constant over time. This version includes the expression for $\Delta R_t (\approx \dot{R}_t)$ from equation III-6:

$$\frac{\Delta P_t}{P_t} = \lambda + \frac{\partial Q_t}{\partial R_t} \left[(W_0 E_t + \sum_{s=1}^{a} v_s E_{t-s})/Q_t \right] \qquad \text{(III-7)}$$

The assumption of constant marginal product of R_t is justified on the grounds that relative to the variance in v_s the trend values of the marginal product of R&D are likely to be stable and the cyclical and other short-term disturbances in it can be allowed for in the process of estimation by introduction of additional variables. Equation III-7 cannot be estimated directly for a single time series because Q_t, which is the denominator of the expenditure-output ratios, would have to change each year with change in t, and a single series does not provide sufficient observations to estimate the weight structure. (It could be estimated when pooled cross section time series observations are available.) Here, for a single sector model the equation is modified by multiplying the equation III-7 by the current year output, Q_t. This nets out the output denominator of the expenditure output ratio on the right-hand side and changes the dependent variable from percentage change in productivity to the dollar value of the productivity change. This is shown in the equation III-8 below:

$$Q_t \frac{\Delta P_t}{P_t} = \lambda Q_t + \frac{\partial Q_t}{\partial R_t} \sum_{s=o}^{a} v_s E_{t-s} \qquad \text{(III-8)}$$

The Gross Stock of Private R&D Capital in Communication

Equation III-8 was estimated statistically with the R&D and total factor productivity data described in Section I. It became necessary in order to stabilize the estimates of the lag structure for cyclical and trend factors to include in this estimate also a time trend factor, $t \cdot Q_t$, and the value of the change in output, ΔQ_t, which is interpreted as a cyclical variable.

Estimates of this equation were made for different lag periods, specifically for a = 10,...15,...20, using different techniques of the distributed lag estimation including the free-form ordinary least squares (OLS), polynomial (Almon) lag structures, and the stochastic constraint Shiller lag method. The best fit estimates of the equation III-8 were obtained for the 17-year lag period. The weights derived by the different lag estimation methods were generally similar. The results for the embodiment period of best fit are shown in Table 4 and in Fig. 1. The polynomial and the Shiller lag structures have a series of negative coefficients in the earlier years with positive, significant, and rising coefficients going back in time to reach peak values in year -8, then diminishing back to zero and turning negative in year -13 and -14, respectively. The structure of the

Table 4

Estimates of a Lag Structure of R&D Effects on the Real Value of Annual Increments in Communication Productivity (Based on the data for 1949-80. Value of output is measured in millions of 1972 dollars.)

Variable	Ordinary Least Squares		Polynomial of 3rd Degree		Shiller Lag	
	Coefficient	t-ratio	Coefficient	t-ratio	Coefficient	t-ratio
Constant	-1479.01	-0.23	3132.51	1.21	266.28	0.11
Output (λ)	0.28	0.28	-0.69	0.88	0.06	0.08
Change in Output Value	0.20	0.39	0.87**	3.57	0.77**	3.06
Time · Output	-0.01	0.39	0.01	0.78	-0.00	0.29
R&D-Output Ratio, Years Lagged						
0	-2.70	1.56	-0.98**	4.03	-1.11**	2.78
1	0.22	0.11	-0.60**	6.68	-0.71*	2.15
2	1.51	1.13	-0.19	1.57	-0.33	1.01
3	-0.01	0.01	0.23**	1.48	-0.00	0.00
4	-3.89	2.13*	0.62**	4.26	0.29	0.78
5	1.00	0.51	0.98**	8.18	0.54	1.45
6	1.30	0.54	1.27**	10.26	0.75*	2.03
7	0.20	0.07	1.48**	8.02	0.88*	2.47
8	-0.24	0.10	1.59**	5.97	0.93**	2.72
9	0.33	0.15	1.57**	4.64	0.89**	2.73
10	0.76	0.33	1.40**	3.68	0.79*	2.36
11	3.87	1.06	1.07**	2.81	0.62	1.60
12	-0.89	0.19	0.55	1.71	0.40	0.81
13	5.53	1.10	0.18	0.90	0.14	0.22
14	-7.36	1.75	-1.14**	9.75	-0.14	0.17
15	10.65	1.30	-2.35**	5.84	-0.47	0.44
16	0.68	0.12	-3.84**	4.53	-0.83	0.63
17	-7.22	1.38	-5.62**	3.93	-1.20	0.75
R^2 Corrected	0.84		0.65		0.60	
D-W Statistic	1.95		2.02		1.94	
Sum of Lag Coefficients	3.72		neg.		1.44	

*Significant at 5 percent level. **Significant at 1 percent level.

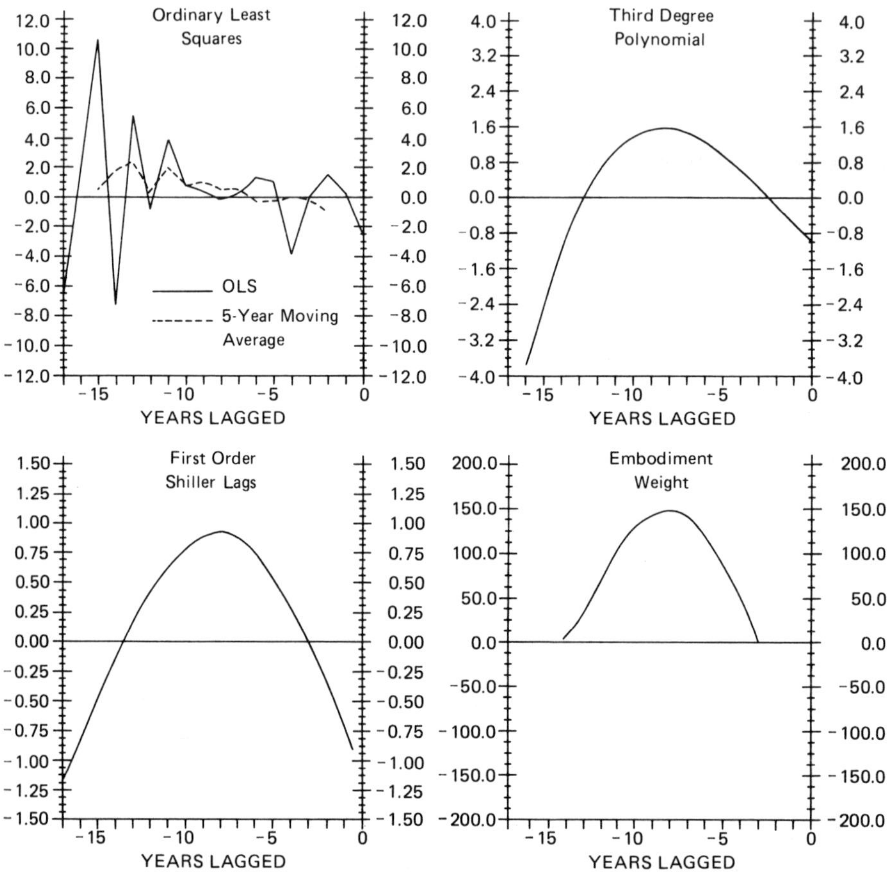

Fig. 1. Distributed lag effects of private R&D expenditure on total factor productivity growth in communication: Coefficients of a 17-year distributed lag structure estimated by different methods

unconstrained OLS coefficients has a longer lag period. Its underlying shape as traced by the five year moving average of the OLS coefficients suggests that the lag structure is positive and further, that the negative values obtained for the years before -15 by the other methods may be the result of the constraining procedures and that the negative values they produced at the beginning of the lag period may be spurious or at least exaggerated. For this reason, the negative early and late coefficients were rejected, and the embodiment lag structure was derived from the positive values of the 17-year Shiller lag fit centered on a series of statistically significant positive lag coefficients in the years (-6) to (-10). This embodiment structure, shown in the bottom right panel of Fig. 1, was used to estimate the capital stock of private R&D in communication and electrical equipment. The capital stock estimates are shown in Table 5.

These estimates should be considered tentative. Other approaches to estimating the embodiment structure should be examined, including perhaps a model that integrates the cyclical and the trend changes with the specification of the embodiment model.

Table 5

Estimated Stock of Private R&D Capital
In Electrical Equipment and Communication, 1948-1980
(in billions of 1972 dollars)*

Year	RD Stock	Year	RD Stock
1948	$ 3.20	1964	$ 10.08
1949	3.44	1965	10.86
1950	3.69	1966	11.71
1951	3.96	1967	12.63
1952	4.24	1968	13.63
1953	4.55	1969	14.70
1954	4.87	1970	15.85
1955	5.23	1971	17.09
1956	5.61	1972	18.42
1957	6.03	1973	19.86
1958	6.48	1974	21.40
1959	6.96	1975	23.07
1960	7.49	1976	24.85
1961	8.06	1977	26.75
1962	8.68	1978	28.75
1963	9.35	1979	30.85
		1980	33.02

*Deflated by the GNP deflator.

Government R&D Capital

The procedure for estimating the embodiment lag coefficient for private R&D was repeated for government R&D expenditures. Because of the limited number of observations available in the existing time series, the estimates of the lag structure for government R&D were made separately from the estimates of lags for the private R&D.

No indication was obtained that a significant embodiment lag structure exists relating government R&D expenditure to communication productivity. Either the government expenditures for R&D performed in electrical equipment and communication industries had no direct effects on productivity of the communication sector or these effects were distributed over a much longer period and could not be detected with the available data and in the presence of interference from the lag effects of private R&D and other sources.

IV. LABOR, FIXED CAPITAL, AND RESEARCH INPUTS IN PRODUCTION

The R&D capital stock estimated with the empirically derived embodiment function is used in analyzing the production relationships in communication. In particular, the possible interactions between R&D capital and the fixed capital stock in this high-technology sector offer an opportunity to examine the possibly joint impact of technological change and of fixed capital formation on productivity. Strong arguments have been advanced (Nelson 1981) in favor of the existence of superadditive and other interactions among productive inputs in generating output. The approach adopted here was in part influenced by these considerations.

The basic form of the production model used here is the variable exponent production function:

$$Q = Ae^{\lambda t} \; L^{(\alpha_0+\alpha_1 R)} \; K^{(\beta_0+\beta_1 R)} \; R^{\gamma} \qquad \text{(IV-1)}$$

In this function, the exponent coefficients defining the elasticity of output with respect to labor (L) and fixed capital (k) inputs may depend positively on the stock of R&D capital (R) and on other variables. This function has the advantage of greater flexibility than the basic Cobb-Douglas function from which it is derived. For example, it allows productive interactions among inputs and non-neutrality of technical change. On the other hand, it requires fewer restrictive assumptions, e.g., about the existence of market equilibria and about the quality of price data than some alternate approaches, notably the approaches based on the dual cost function.

Previous research (Nadiri and Shankerman 1980) has found that the technological change in the communication industry has not been neutral. That study was based on an estimate of a translog production function. Translog estimation requires availability of reliable price data, which are not available for the communication sector as a whole. The estimation strategy adopted here for dealing with non-neutrality in a log-additive production function consists of estimating variable elasticity coefficients where the research capital R is employed to determine these coefficients. Hence, if a change in R changes the coefficient of L or K, it means it changes the marginal product of L or K. At present, the results of a nonstochastic variable coefficients model are reported. In the future, it may be possible to explore the stochastic estimation of the model with variable coefficients with own error terms.

In the specific production function postulated here, the R&D capital enters the production process in two ways: first as a neutral independent stock with its own elasticity exponent and again as a determinant of the marginal products and hence elasticities of labor and capital. This production function, cited in equation IV-1, also has a disembodied time and trend given by λ.

Initial estimates of equation IV-1 did not produce any significant coefficients for the disembodied time trend, and it was dropped in subsequent analysis. Similarly, no significant estimates were obtained for the neutral term β_0, of the exponent of the fixed capital stock. Its estimates were consistently not significant and often were negative. It was also dropped from further analysis.

Consistently positive and highly significant estimates were obtained for the parameters α_0, the neutral coefficient in the exponent of labor, and γ, the elasticity of output with respect to research capital. Some significant and positive estimates were obtained for β_1, which relates R&D stock to the marginal product of fixed capital stock. This suggests a probable interaction between research capital and fixed capital. Positive estimates of α_1 were also obtained, but when research capital was included in the exponents of both labor and fixed capital, neither of the two parameters, α_1 or β_1, was significant. Based on the judgment that the results of R&D are much more likely to be embodied in fixed capital stock than in labor, it was decided to omit α_1 and to retain β_1 in the production function estimation. The results of the following best fit equation

$$Q = AL^{\alpha_0} K^{\beta_1 R} R^{\gamma} \qquad \text{(IV-2)}$$

estimated in logarithms by the GLS method are shown in Table 6.

This equation had consistent estimates for the period 1948-80 and for the two subperiods. All estimated coefficients were significant at least at the 5 percent level, except the coefficient β_1, in the two subperiods, especially in the period 1948-63. The estimates of the parameters for labor and for research capital are similar in the three periods. Generally, all the results obtained for the subperiod 1964-80 are qualitatively similar to the results obtained for the entire period 1948-80. The elasticity coefficient for hours is not too different from the share of labor in value-added, which averaged 50 percent in communication during the period 1948-80. The coefficient, β_1, estimated as the regression coefficient of RlnK, is highly significant for the entire period and is almost significant at 5 percent and of similar size (0.001) for the later subperiod. No significant estimate of β_1 was obtained for the earlier subperiod 1948-63.

The coefficient of research capital, γ, is highly significant, large, and of similar size in all three cases. The elasticity coefficients for R&D are quite large in comparison with most estimates of elasticity of fixed or R&D capital, but for the very R&D-intensive communication sector they may be within a reasonable range. The ratio of private R&D capital to output in communication averaged about 0.6 in both subperiods. The implied marginal product of R&D capital is then 1.5 and 1.25. Interpreted as productivity rates of return to R&D embodied in the R&D stock, of 125 - 150 percent these marginal products, though quite different in concept, are not much higher than the rates obtained by researchers as industry cross-

Table 6

Logarithmic Estimates of the Production Function for Communication
GLS estimates of the equation $\ln Q = \ln A + \alpha_0 \ln L + \beta_1 (R \ln K) + \gamma \ln R$
(t-ratios in parentheses)

Parameter	1948-80	1948-63	1964-80
lnA	-4.936** (58.19)	-5.522** (11.10)	-4.461** (6.85)
α 0	0.411** (8.63)	0.304** (3.60)	0.476** (4.78)
β 1	0.00078** (4.65)	-0.0018 (0.78)	0.0011 (2.01)
γ	0.805** (70.73)	0.886** (13.13)	0.748** (9.75)
R^2 (Corrected)	1.000	1.000	1.000
Durbin-Watson Statistic	1.94	2.16	1.76

**Statistically significant at 1 percent level.

section coefficients for lagged R&D and about twice the internal rates of return to total investment in innovation (of which R&D is almost one-half) estimated directly in case studies.

Since the R&D data are generally better for years after 1953 when the NSF industry surveys were begun, and especially after 1957 when they were redesigned, perhaps too much weight should not be given to the estimates obtained for the earlier subperiod. On the other hand, the productive relationships of the industry may have undergone a change between the two subperiods and the positive influence of the R&D capital on the productivity of fixed capital did increase with time.

One more attempt was made to test the possibility that government-funded R&D has had a direct impact on the productivity of the communication sector. Because, as reported in Section III, no distributed lag structure could be identified to derive a productivity embodiment period for government R&D, a stock of cumulated government expenditures for R&D performed in the electrical equipment and communication industries lagged 10 years was added to the equations estimated in Table 6. However, no statistical indications were obtained of a positive effect of this stock on the productivity of the communication sector. Thus, it appears that the principal economic impact of government-funded R&D, performed in the electrical equipment and communication industries, taken in the aggregate, may be in the form of transferring the results of this R&D to the private sector by expanding the technology base and thus stimulating additional private R&D investment in those industries, along the lines discussed in Section II above.

V. PRICE OF COMMUNICATION OUTPUT

Effects of Productivity and Regulation

Economic research has established that changes in prices of products of individual industries have been correlated negatively with changes in productivity of these industries, especially with changes in total factor productivity, which accounts for both labor and capital inputs (Kendrick 1961; Kendrick and Grossman 1980).

Thus, industries with large productivity increases have had slow rates of price increase (or in periods of general price decline largest declines) and vice versa. The reason is that increases in total factor productivity represent increases in productive efficiency and hence reductions in real costs of production, which should lead to reductions in price. This process is expected to work especially well in competitive industries, but the negative relationship between productivity and price has been observed also in regulated industries. Thus, one determinant of price of the communication output to be considered is productivity of the communication sector.

In analyzing the price trends of the individual sectors of the economy, relative prices are relevant, i.e., prices of the given output relative to other prices in the economy. The present analysis is conducted in terms of trends in the price of the net output of the communication sector (Pc) relative to the price of the net output of the total private business economy (P). Both prices are measured by the respective implicit price deflators for the net output defined by the U.S. Department of Commerce. Their ratio (Pc/P) is the dependent variable, an index with 1972=1.0.

The negative relationship between relative productivity of an industry and the relative price of its output is highly nonlinear. The reason is the asymmetry between the theoretically unlimited magnitudes of increases and the possible magnitudes of declines, which are limited to 100 percent. It is more convenient, therefore, to estimate the expected linear relationship between the inverse of productivity, i.e., the relative unit input and the relative price. This approach is adopted here.

The relative unit input index used is the ratio of the input index based on work hours and fixed capital inputs to the index of net output in the communication sector (UIc) divided by the corresponding ratio of input and output indexes for the business economy (UI). The component indexes developed by Elliot S. Grossman and John W. Kendrick at the American Productivity Center, rebased to 1972=1.00, are used here to calculate the relative unit input index for communication (UIc/UI).

Throughout the period analyzed here, 1948-80, the price of telecommunication, which constitutes most of the output of the communication sector, has been regulated by federal and state commissions. In the present analysis, no prior assumption is made about regulatory behavior. However, the hypothesis is tested that the price of communication has been positively related to the capital-output ratio. The rationale is that the telecommunication industry may have expanded its capital stock beyond the competitively optimal point because the regulatory bodies have been granting rate increases based on the concept of a, possibly constant, fair rate of return on capital. This hypothesis is tested here by introducing the ratio of fixed capital stock (which accounts for most of the capital invested in communication) to output (K/Q) in the estimating equation for price of the communication. The effect of the capital-output ratio is not significant in from the estimates by Grossman and Kendrick.

The following price equation is then estimated for the communication sector:

$$(Pc/P = ao + a1(K/Q) + a2(UIc/UI)$$

where for all price and relative input indexes 1972=1.0, and both capital stock and output in the ratio, K/Q, are measured in constant prices.

Estimates of the Price Equation

Estimates of the price equation for the net output of the communication sector obtained by the generalized least squares (GLS) method for the entire period 1948-80 and for the two subperiods 1948-66 and 1964-80, are shown in Table 7. These results show striking differences between the subperiods, clearly suggesting that the period 1948-80 is not homogeneous. Separate subperiod equations are needed to describe properly the price trends in communication. The effect of the capital labor ratio is not significant in any of the estimates. All its coefficients are very small and negative. The subperiod equations were reestimated without the capital-output ratio, producing essentially the same results for the remaining factors.

In the first subperiod, the relative price has been constant, and neither the capital output ratio nor the relative unit input had any statistically significant effect on it. In contrast, in the second subperiod, the relative price of the communication output is completely explainable by the relative unit input index.

The absence of any apparent effect of the capital-output ratio on price of communication output throws serious doubt on the hypothesis that the capital stock was overexpanded in communication. The sharp split in the statistical explanation of the price of communication output suggests a different interpretation. In the first subperiod, the relative price varied very little, while the general price level given by the implicit deflator for the output of the private economy increased by 40 percent from 1948 to 1963. It is possible that during that time the telecommunication utilities have been requesting and the regulators have been granting "general cost of living" rate increases, i.e., increases equivalent to general price inflation. The relative price of communication was not influenced by the relative productivity increases. It remained constant in spite of relative decline in unit inputs at an annual rate of 3.2 percent.

In the second subperiod, the relative productivity increases in communication have been more than fully reflected in the relative price declines. Relative unit inputs declined at an annual rate of 2.1 percent, and the

Table 7

Price Equation for Communication Output
GLS estimates of the equation $P_c/P + a_o + a_1(K/Q) + a_2(UI_c/UI)$
(t-ratios in parentheses)

Regression Coefficient	1948-80	1948-63		1964-80	
a_o	0.703** (5.03)	1.350** (7.54)	1.182** (24.52)	-0.311** (3.02)	-0.298** (3.08)
a_1	-0.000 (0.48)	-0.055 (1.02)		-0.001 (0.62)	
a_2	0.235* (2.74)	0.027 (0.853)	0.015 (0.44)	1.322** (12.71)	1.301** (20.94)
R^2 (Corrected)	0.918	0.065	0.449	0.986	0.983
D-W Statistic	1.98	1.70	1.64	1.70	1.66

*Statistically significant at 5 percent level.
**Statistically significant at 1 percent level.

relative price of communication declined at 3.2 percent. Clearly, there has been a change in the pricing of the communication output, but the reasons for this are not obvious. In particular, the effects of changes in technology, in competitive environment of the communication industry, in price behavior of firms, and in the behavior of regulators would need to be examined.

Some of the technical aspects of this analysis should be tested in the future. It remains to be established whether the results depend on the concepts and data used here. In particular, the sensitivity of the results with respect to measurement of the fixed capital stock, measurement of the labor input by unweighted work hours, and the choice of the total factor productivity formula should be examined.

VI. DEMAND FOR COMMUNICATION OUTPUT

The standard variables employed in analysis of demand are price and income. Thus, a demand function may be specified in which the quantity of output of communication is a constant elasticity function of the relative price of communication and of the GNP, which represents the real income of the economy:

$$Q_c = A(P_c/P)^{\alpha} \quad (GNP)^{\beta} \qquad \text{(VI-1)}$$

Because the structural change reflected in the increasing use of computers may also have generated additional demand for communication, the number of computers in use in the United States is added to this equation. The data for computers is obtained from a study by Phister (1979, 247, 601), who compiled a time series of the number of computers in use in the United States for the years 1956-1978, based largely on his own estimates for the years 1959-1978. The number of computers is introduced into the demand equation with a two-year lag:

$$Q_c = A(P_c/P)^{\alpha} \quad (GNP)^{\beta}[C(-2)]^{\gamma} \qquad \text{(VI-2)}$$

The lag is justified by the existence of an absorption period between acquisition and full operation of new equipment by the firms similar to that estimated for the new types of aircraft (Terleckyj 1982b). It is also necessary because no computer data are available for later years. The use of two-year lag was tested by performing equation estimates for a period ending in 1978 with and without the lag. The results were essentially the same. It is probably not feasible to extend the series of computers in use in a meaningful way because of the large change in the nature of computers. After 1978, the series would become progressively dominated by the microcomputers.

The equation VI-2 containing a constant elasticity parameter for computer use can be estimated statistically only for the second subperiod, 1964-80, because the number of computers in use is zero in the years 1955 and before. Hence, no logarithmic estimates can be made of this equation for the first subperiod. However, constant elasticity formulation is only one way, and perhaps not the best one, to introduce computer use into the demand analysis.

Structural changes may be represented by a constant time trend which would account for an additional growth component of the communication output not explainable by price and income, such as growth resulting from increased international demand for communication and from increased demand for communication by computers. The demand equation is then specified as:

$$Q_c = Ae^{\lambda t} \ (P_c/P)^{\alpha} \ (GNP)^{\beta} \qquad \text{(VI-3)}$$

Two equations were estimated for the entire period and one for the second subperiod. The results are summarized in Table 8. Significant estimates were obtained for equation VI-1 indicating relatively high GNP elasticity of 1.67 in the first subperiod and still rather high 1.17 in the second. A relatively high estimate of price elasticity of -1.23 was obtained in the second subperiod in which there has been considerable price decline. For the first subperiod, in which the relative price of communication output change very little, no significant estimates of price elasticity were obtained, though the estimated price coefficient has the expected negative sign. In this instance, the results obtained by the OLS and GLS techniques were at variance with the results obtained by robust estimating techniques. Generalized least absolute deviations and generalized biweighted least squares techniques produced price elasticity estimates of -1.14 and -0.91, respectively, for the first subperiod.

Table 8

Demand Function for Communication Output
GLS estimates of the equation
$\ln Qc = a_0 + a_1 \ln(P_c/P) + a_2 \ln(GNP) + a_3 \ln(C_{-2})$

Regression Coefficient	1948-80	1948-63	1964-80	
a_0	-8.44** (17.49)	-9.01** (12.12)	-4.97** (3.82)	-0.32 (.20)
a^1	-0.765** (5.35)	-0.180 (0.45)	-1.230** (6.28)	0.501 (2.05)
a_2	1.667** (23.65)	1.740** (14.94)	1.173 (6.31)	0.392 (1.52)
a_3				0.215** (3.63)
R^2 (Corrected)	0.980	0.976	0.993	0.996
D-W Statistic	1.93	1.98	1.95	1.94

**Significant at 1 percent level.

When a separate time trend was introduced in the estimates of equation VI-3, very large regression coefficients were obtained for time, and the coefficients for price and for GNP elasticity were much reduced. However, the simple correlation between logarithm of GNP and time was 1.000. Because of this multicollinearity, no meaningful estimation of a separate autonomous time trend was possible. A similar result, and apparently for the same reason, was obtained for the second subperiod when the logarithm of the number of computers was introduced, as is shown in the last column of Table 8. The logarithm of time series of computers in use is perfectly correlated with the logarithm of GNP.

Equation VI-2 was reformulated making use of the definition of the elasticity term for computers in equation VI-2, γ, as the product of the marginal demand for communication per computer unit and the ratio of computers to the demand for communication: $\gamma = (dQc/dC)(C/Qc)$. The ratio of computers to communication output was then treated as a factor of the dependent variable and the following "constant marginal demand" model was estimated:

$$\ln Q_c = a_o + a_1 \ln(P_c/P) + a_2 \ln GNP + a_3 [(C/Q_c)\ln C] \qquad \text{(VI-4)}$$

No significant estimates were obtained for the term a3. The estimates of other parameters were similar to those obtained in equation VI-1.

While the increasing use of computers undoubtedly contributed to growth in the demand for communication output, it seems impossible to isolate this effect with the available series of the number of computers in use. Probably the nature of computers has been changing too much to permit capturing this effect statistically. Other available data such as the undeflated value of computers in use, etc., appear equally unpromising. Perhaps, the total communication output should also be disaggregated and the separate data for the communication by computers used in the analysis. In any event, better measurement of computer use is needed, perhaps in terms of the number of persons engaged in computer work, but such data are not available at this time.

VII. SUMMARY AND CONCLUSIONS

In this paper, the patterns of growth of the communication industry are explored by estimating a series of interdependent relationships that link such factors influencing growth of the communication industry as the private investment in communication R&D, production and productivity of communication, price of communication, demand for communication output, government spending for communication R&D, and the general economic conditions. Together these relationships form a model of growth of the communications sector. The model was estimated for the period 1948-80 and for two subperiods, 1948-63 and 1964-80. The results differed between subperiods. Following are the GLS estimates of the key relationships for the period 1964-80:

$$RDc(0) = \underset{(1.11)}{-362.03} + \underset{(15.87)}{.054}\ Qc(-1) - \underset{(3.08)}{61.77}\ U(0) + \underset{(5.69)}{.560}\ GRDc(-2) \qquad \text{(VII-1)}$$

$$\begin{aligned} Rc(0) = {} & .046\ RDc(-4) + .133\ RDc(-5) + .253\ RDc(-6) \qquad \text{(VII-2)} \\ & + .394\ RDc(-7) + .543\ RDc(-8) + .686\ RD(-9) \\ & + .813\ RDc(-10) + .913\ RDc(-11) + .977\ RDc(-12) \\ & + \sum_{t=-\infty}^{-13} RDc(t) \end{aligned}$$

$$\ln Qc = \underset{(6.85)}{-4.461} + \underset{(4.78)}{.476}\ \ln L + \underset{(2.01)}{.0011}\ (R \cdot \ln K) + \underset{(+9.75)}{.748}\ \ln Rc \qquad \text{(VII-3)}$$

$$Pc/P = \underset{(3.08)}{-2.98} + \underset{(20.94)}{1.301}\ (UIc/UI) \qquad \text{(VII-4)}$$

$$\ln Qc = \underset{(3.82)}{-4.97} - \underset{(6.28)}{1.230}\ \ln(Pc/P) + \underset{(6.31)}{1.173}\ \ln(GNP) \qquad \text{(VII-5)}$$

(The numbers in parentheses next to the variable denote the year where lagged relations are estimated, and the numbers in parentheses listed under the coefficients are their t-ratios.)

Here, private investment in communication and electrical equipment R&D depends in a large measure, more than in the first subperiod, on previous government expenditure for R&D in communication and electrical equipment and also on the output of communication and the general economic conditions (VII-1). The stock of private R&D capital, Rc, consists of all past private R&D expenditures lagged 13 years or more and of increasing proportions of R&D expenditure lagged four to 12 years (VII-2). The communication output, Qc, depends on the research and development capital in a major way directly and through its interaction with the fixed capital as well as on labor and fixed capital inputs (VII-3). The price of the communication output in this period depends on the relative unit input (the inverse of total factor productivity) in communication (VII-4). The demand for the communication output has been a function both of its relative price, especially in the second subperiod, and of the size of the economy (VII-5).

In this model, the exogenous variables represent government policy and the state of the economy. Government expenditure for communication R&D is the only policy variable in the above system. Attempts to model regulatory behavior by means of independent variables were not successful. Also, the attempt to introduce technical change exogenously by including a time series for the number of computers in use did not produce significant results. The state of the economy is given by the GNP and the unemployment rate, U. Here, labor, l, and fixed capital, K, employed in communication are also listed as given, but conceptually they could be derived endogenously from equations VII-3 and VII-5. All other variables are endogenous to the model. However, the total factor productivity used in estimating price is not conceptually consistent with the production function estimated for the communication which contains a component reflecting interdependence between fixed capital and R&D capital. The decision was made in this study to explore the structure of the production function directly. Development of an internally consistent treatment of production and productivity functions is a task for future research.

A number of other questions discussed in the preceding sections remain to be settled. This includes the possible existence of autonomous time trends, especially in demand for communication and the specific formulation of the production function. In addition, of course, there are a number of questions of data specification and of the level of aggregation as well as of the choice of the proper base period for each relationship. At the econometric level are the questions of choice of the estimating techniques for identifying the relationships in the model and the need for testing the estimates by joing estimation of at least some relationships where sufficient data are available.

The model presented here is viewed as a beginning step towards further development and eventual testing of a consistent growth model for its predictive power, both for the period for which it has been estimated and over the years beyond it.

Another important issue that should be addressed at a later time is the interdependence between the communication sector and the rest of the economy. Of course, the communication sector itself is a part of the total economy and thus contributes to its growth. But, some statistical indications have been obtained, beyond this effect, that both communication output and computer use may be directly related to the growth of productivity in the economy. Ultimately, it should be possible to integrate the growth model of the communication sector with the growth model of the economy, and possibly with models for other sectors as well, in a coherent system that would permit tracing of the effects of technical change and other sources of growth between sectors, in particular, between the sectors which originate technological change and other sources of growth between sectors, in particular between the sectors which originate technological change and the sectors which use the results of this change.

NOTES

I would like to thank David M. Levy for numerous suggestions and discussions of the material presented here and for help in developing the underlying econometric analyses; Robert E. Evenson, Martin K. Holdrich, Leonid Hurwicz, Albert N. Link, Larry E. Ruff, and John T. Scott for many helpful comments and suggestions; and Elliot S. Grossman and John W. Kendrick for providing their detailed input, output, and productivity data for the private business economy, its sectors and industries. I alone am responsible for the remaining errors. The research presented in this paper was supported by grant IST-8119070 from the National Science Foundation Division of Information Science and Technology.

REFERENCES

1 Evenson, R.E., A Century of Productivity Change in U.S. Agriculture: An Analysis of the Role of Invention, Research and Extension. Center Discussion Paper no. 296, Yale University (August 1978).

2 Goldberg, L., The Influence of Federal R&D Funding on the Demand for and Returns to Industrial R&D, CRC 388/1979 (Public Research Institute, Center for Naval Analysis, Alexandria, 1979).

3 Griliches, Z., Hybrid corn: An exploration in the economics of technological change, Econometrica 25, no. 4 (1957) 501-522.

4 Griliches, Z. and Lichtenberg, F., R&D and Productivity at the Industry Level; Is There Still a Relationship? Working Paper Series no. 850, National Bureau of Economic Research, Inc. (February 1982).

5 Kendrick, J.W., Productivity Trends in the United States. Princeton: Princeton University Press. 1961.

6 Kendrick, J.W. and Grossman, E.S., Productivity in the United States: Trends and Cycles (The John Hopkins University Press, Baltimore, 1980).

7 Levin, R.C. and Reiss, P.C., Tests of a Schumpetrian Model of R&D and Market Structure. Paper prepared for the BNER Conference on R&D, Patents, and Productivity, Lenox, Mass. (October 2-4, 1981).

8 Levy, D.M., Robust Regression Under Conditions of Normality and Frequent Autocorrelation. Unpublished manuscript (November 1983).

9 Levy, D.M. and Terleckyj, N.E., Effects of Government R&D on Private R&D Investment and Productivity: A Macroeconomic Analysis. Paper given at the annual meetings of the Southern Economic Association, Atlanta, November 11, 1982. Bell Journal of Economics (Fall 1983) 551-61.

10 Link, A.N. An analysis of the composition of R&D spending, Southern Economic Journal (October 1982) 342-49.

11 Mansfield, E., Industrial Research and Technological Innovation; An Econometric Analysis (W.W. Norton, New York, 1968).

12 Mansfield, E. and Switzer, L., Effects of Federal Support on Company-Financed R and D: The Case of Energy. Paper delivered at the annual meetings of the Southern Economic Association, Atlanta (November 11, 1982).

13 Nadiri, I.M. and Shankerman, M.A., The structure of production, technological change, and the rate of growth of total factor productivity in the Bell system, in: Cowing, T. and Stevenson, R. (eds.), Productivity Measurement in Regulated Industries (Academic Press, New York, 1980).

14 Nelson, R.R., Research on productivity growth and productivity differences: Dead ends and new departures, Journal of Economic Literature 19 (September 1981) 1029-1064.

15 Phister, M., Jr., Data Processing Technology and Economics (Santa Monica Publishing Company and Digital Press, Santa Monica, 1979).

16 Scott, J.T., Firm Versus Industry Variability in R&D Intensity. NBER Conference on R&D, Patents, and Productivity, Lenox, Mass. (October 2-4, 1981).

THE CONTRIBUTORS

WILLIAM J. BAUMOL, a native of New York City, received his B.S.S. degree in 1942 from the College of the City of New York and his Ph.D. from the University of London in 1949. He is professor of economics at Princeton University (since 1954) and New York University (since 1971). He has received many honors, including a Guggenheim Fellowship in 1957-58, a Ford Faculty Fellowship in 1965-66, election to the American Academy of Arts and Sciences in 1971, and selection as a distinguished fellow of the American Economic Association in 1982. He has also held many important professional positions, including founding member and member of the board of directors of the World Resources Institute, membership on the Research Advisory Board of Resources for the Future, the research advisory board of the Committee for Economic Development, the Committee on Research of the American Philosophical Society, the editorial advisory board of *The Supreme Court Economic Review*, and the board of trustees of the Joint Council on Economic Education. He is a fellow of the Econometric Society and a past president of the American Economic Association, the Eastern Economic Association, and the Association of Environmental and Resource Economists. He has served as vice-president of the American Association of University Professors and on the editorial boards of numerous scholarly journals, including the *American Economic Review*, the *Journal of Economic Literature*, and *Management Science*. Professor Baumol has published numerous articles and more than a dozen books.

YALE M. BRAUNSTEIN is an associate professor at the School of Library and Information Studies of the University of California, Berkeley. Professor Braunstein received his doctorate in economics from Stanford University. Prior to his appointment at Berkeley, he was a member of the economics faculties at New York and Brandeis universities. Professor Braunstein's current research interests include the market structure of information and communications industries, the economics of intellectual property rights, and regulatory issues.

CHEE-WAH CHEAH is a research fellow at the Institute of Culture and Communication, East-West Center, Honolulu, Hawaii. He is a graduate of the University of Malaya, Kuala Lumpur (B. Economics, Honours) and the University of Hawaii (Ph.D., economics). Prior to his graduate studies in the United States, he was an economic analyst in a private consulting firm in Kuala Lumpur. He also served as a teaching assistant in economics at the University of Hawaii before joining the East-West Center. His current research deals with the economics of regulation, with particular reference to the area of computer communications and transborder data flows.

CHARLES JONSCHER is an economist at the Massachusetts Institute of Technology, where he is co-director of the Research Program on Communications Policy. He is also co-founder and executive vice-president of CSP International, a New York and London consulting firm that studies the communications industries. He has degrees in electrical engineering from Cambridge University and economics from Harvard University. Dr. Jonscher's research covers various topics in the economics of information and communications. He has recently produced an economic model that identifies the productivity of the information sector and assesses the implications of information technology for overall business performance. He also studies the structure and regulation of the telecommunications industry.

MEHEROO JUSSAWALLA is a research economist at the East-West Center Institute of Culture and Communication. Before migrating to the United States in 1975, she was professor of economics and dean of the faculty of social sciences at Osmania University, Hyderabad, India. She has served on the research programs committee of the Planning Commission, Government of India, and on the board of directors of the State Bank of India. She has had several awards for visiting professorships in the United States at Hood College, Vassar, Elmira, and Cedar Crest. From 1975 to 1977 she was professor of economics at St. Mary's College, Maryland. Her research at the East-West Center covers information and communication economics at the national and international levels. She is currently focusing her research on information sector studies for Pacific countries. He publications in professional journals include articles on the economics of telecommunications technology, economics of development communications, and transborder data flows. She is editor of the journal Information Economics and Policy and is the author of The Economics of Communication (Pergamon, 1981), Communications Economics and Development (co-edited, Pergamon, 1982), and Dynamics of Economic Development (University Microfilms International, 1980).

D.M. LAMBERTON is professor of economics at the University of Queensland, Australia. He is the author of Share Price Indices in Australia, The Theory of Profit, and Science, Technology and the Australian Economy and co-author of Economic Effects of the Australian Patent System. He edited or co-edited the following books: Industrial Economics, Economics of Information and Knowledge, The Information Revolution, Communication Economics and Development, and The Trouble with Technology. He is an editor of Information Economics and Policy and Prometheus and a member of the editorial board of Telecommunications Policy. Professor Lamberton has served as a consultant to governments and international agencies, including the OECD and UNESCO.

RICHARD N. LANGLOIS received the B.A. degree from Williams College in 1974, the M.S. degree from Yale University in 1975, and the M.S. and Ph.D. degrees from Stanford University in 1976 and 1981, respectively. He taught for three years at New York University, where he was affiliated both with the Economics Department at Washington Square and with the Graduate School of Business Administration. He is now assistant professor of economics at the University of Connecticut, Storrs.

LAWRENCE PULLEY received his Ph.D in economics from the University of Virginia and is assistant professor of economics at Brandeis University, where he joined the faculty in 1978. His current research interests include applied microeconomic theory and statistical applications in finance.

NESTOR E. TERLECKYJ is a vice-president of the National Planning Association and director of its Center for Socio-Economic Analysis. He holds a Ph.D. degree in economics from Columbia University and is the author of several books and numerous articles in the fields of economic growth, productivity, and economics of technical and social change. Dr. Terleckyj has previously held professional positions with the U.S. Office of Management and Budget, the Conference Board, and the National Bureau of Economic Research, Inc.

EDWARD N. WOLFF is an associate professor of economics at New York University. He received his undergraduate training in economics at Harvard College from 1964 through 1968 and his graduate training at Yale University from 1970 to 1974. He has been teaching at New York University since 1974 and also worked as a research associate at the National Bureau of Economic Research from 1974 to 1977. His current research interests fall into three areas. The first is the analysis of productivity growth trends in the United States, with special focus on the role of research and development and compositional effects. The second is the study of wealth distribution and the wealth accumulation process of the household sector. The third area concerns the macroeconomic relations between capital accumulation, productivity growth, the class distribution of income, and unproductive labor.